I NEED TO BE MY AUTHENTIC SELF!

Guiding Leaders To Live Purpose-Driven Careers

Dr. T. Austin

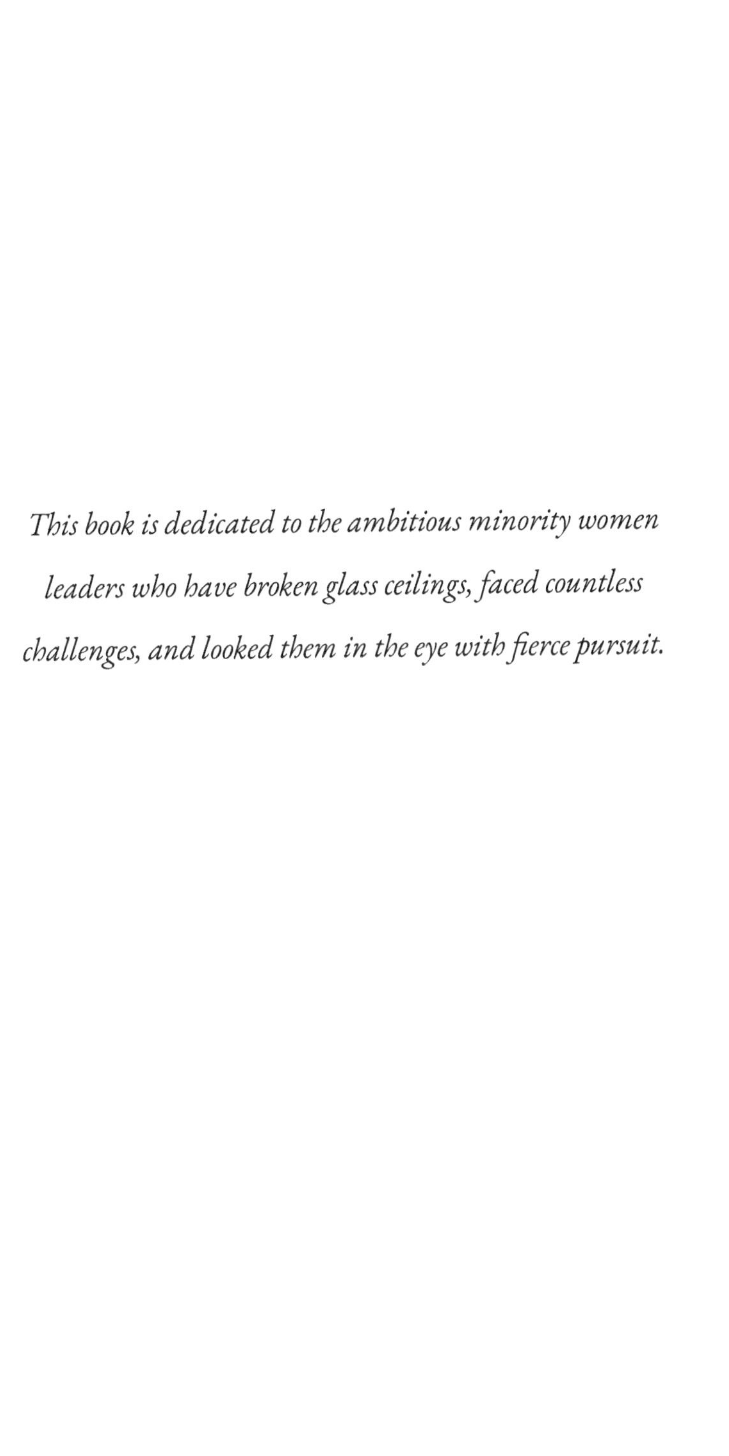

This book is dedicated to the ambitious minority women leaders who have broken glass ceilings, faced countless challenges, and looked them in the eye with fierce pursuit.

TABLE OF CONTENTS

INTRODUCTION UNVEILING THE DREAM i
Discovering Your God-Given Purpose..ii
The Importance of Faith in Pursuing Your Career Goals iii
The Journey Ahead: What to Expect from This Book v
CHAPTER ONE 1
Navigating the Challenges of Being a Minority Woman in
Management 7
Overcoming Stereotypes and Biases in the Workplace...........14
Real-Life Stories of Minority Women Who Have Succeeded in
Leadership Roles 21
CHAPTER TWO..29
Cultural Barriers And The African American Experience..........29
Understanding the Unique Cultural Challenges Faced by African
American Women..29
Strategies for Breaking Through Cultural Barriers in Your Career
....33
Celebrating the Strengths and Contributions of African American
Women in the Workplace 38
CHAPTER THREE 46
Tapping Into Faith..46
How Faith Can Guide and Strengthen You in Your Career
Journey 46
Biblical Principles for Success and Leadership 48
Developing a Strong Prayer Life and Relationship with God ...51
CHAPTER FOUR...57
Embracing God's Spirit...57
Understanding That God Did Not Give Us a Spirit of Fear (2
Timothy 1:7) 57
Practical Ways to Overcome Fear and Step into Your Purpose
....63
The Role of Faith in Building Confidence and Courage...........75
CHAPTER FIVE 80
Conducting A SWOT Analysis On Yourself.............................80
The Importance of Self-Awareness in Career Growth 80
How to Identify Your Strengths, Weaknesses, Opportunities, and
Threats 83
Identify Your Strengths 84
Identify Your Weaknesses 86
Identify Your Opportunities 88
Some questions to ask yourself:...89
Identify Your Threats 91
Some questions to ask yourself:...92

Using Your SWOT Analysis to Create a Personal Development Plan 95
CHAPTER SIX 105
Writing Your "Self-Contract"...105
Setting Goals and Commitments to Yourself and Your Career 106
Aligning Your Self-Contract with God's Purpose for Your Life 110
Holding Yourself Accountable to Your Self-Contract.............113
CHAPTER SEVEN..120
Trusting That God Directs Your Steps and Purpose (Proverbs 16:9) 121
Discerning God's Will Through Prayer, Scripture, and Wise Counsel 127
How to Seek and Follow God's guidance in Your Career Decisions..137
CHAPTER EIGHT 142
Let Your Feet Do The Walking And Your Mind Do The Talking 142
Taking Action Steps to Bring Your Vision to Life 143
The Power of Positive Self-Talk and Affirmations 147
Overcoming Procrastination and Maintaining Momentum 152
CHAPTER NINE 162
Becoming A Leader Of Influence..162
Developing Your Leadership Skills as a Minority Woman......163
Using Your Influence to Inspire and Empower Others 167
Servant Leadership: Leading with Humility and Grace..........171
CHAPTER TEN...182
Overcoming Obstacles With Faith And Resilience 182
Strategies for Dealing with Setbacks and Challenges in Your Career 183
How to Maintain Faith and Resilience in the Face of Adversity 187
Finding Strength in Your Identity in Christ 192
CONCLUSION 202
Embracing Your God-Given Purpose 202
Reflecting on Your Journey and Growth 202
Encouragement to Continue Pursuing Your Career Purpose with Faith and Confidence 204
Final thoughts and blessings for the road ahead...................214
Acknowledgements 226
About the Author 228

INTRODUCTION
UNVEILING THE DREAM

As I embarked on my journey as a minority woman in leadership, I found myself grappling with a myriad of challenges and uncertainties. It was a path riddled with obstacles, stereotypes, and cultural barriers that often left me feeling overwhelmed and discouraged. However, amidst the struggles, I discovered the transformative power of faith and the importance of aligning my career aspirations with the purpose God had destined for my life.

In this book, I invite you to join me on a journey of self-discovery, empowerment, and unwavering faith as we navigate the complexities of being minority women in leadership roles. Together, we will explore the struggles we face, the cultural barriers we must overcome, and the invaluable role that our Christian faith plays in guiding us towards our God-given purpose.

Discovering Your God-Given Purpose

One of the most fundamental questions we ask ourselves is, "What is my purpose in life?" It is a question that transcends career goals and personal aspirations, striking at the core of our very existence. As minority women, we often find ourselves at the intersection of various identities, roles, and expectations, making it all the more challenging to discern our true calling.

However, I firmly believe that each one of us has a unique, God-given purpose—a divine blueprint for our lives that goes beyond our professional titles and societal roles. It is a purpose rooted in our identity as children of God, created in His image and imbued with distinct talents, passions, and experiences.

Discovering your God-given purpose is a journey of self-reflection, prayer, and attentiveness to the stirrings of your heart. It involves seeking God's guidance through His word, listening to the promptings of the Holy Spirit, and stepping out in faith to pursue the path He has set before you.

Throughout this book, we will delve into practical strategies and biblical principles that will help you uncover your unique purpose and align your career goals with God's plan for your life. We will explore the importance of conducting a thorough self-assessment, identifying your strengths, weaknesses, opportunities, and threats (SWOT), and crafting a "self-contract" that reflects your commitment to your God-given purpose.

The Importance of Faith in Pursuing Your Career Goals

As minority women in leadership, we often face a plethora of challenges that can easily discourage us and cause us to question our abilities and worth. From systemic barriers and discrimination to imposter syndrome and self-doubt, the road to success can be fraught with obstacles that threaten to derail our progress.

However, it is in these moments of adversity that our faith becomes our anchor, providing us with the strength, resilience, and wisdom to persevere. Faith is the bedrock upon which we build our careers and the lens through which we interpret our experiences.

When we tap into the power of our Christian faith, we gain access to a wellspring of divine guidance, empowerment, and peace. We recognize that our ultimate source of strength and direction comes from God, who has promised to never leave us nor forsake us (Deuteronomy 31:6).

Throughout this book, we will explore how faith can serve as a catalyst for overcoming fear, embracing our God-given identity, and walking in the purpose He has ordained for our lives. We will examine biblical examples of women who exemplified faith in their leadership roles and glean insights from their experiences.

By anchoring our career pursuits in faith, we position ourselves to receive God's favor, wisdom, and direction. We learn to trust in His timing, lean on His strength, and find comfort in the knowledge that He is working all things together for our good and His glory (Romans 8:28).

The Journey Ahead: What to Expect from This Book

As you embark on this journey of discovering your God-given purpose and pursuing your career goals with faith, I invite you to approach this book with an open heart and a willingness to grow. The path ahead may not be easy, but it is a path paved with purpose, empowerment, and the unwavering support of a loving God.

In the chapters that follow, we will delve into the unique challenges faced by minority women in leadership, including cultural barriers, stereotypes, and biases. We will explore practical strategies for navigating these obstacles and celebrate the strengths and contributions of minority women in the workplace.

We will also examine the transformative power of faith in shaping our leadership journey. From developing a strong prayer life and relationship with God to applying biblical principles for success and leadership, we will discover how faith can guide and strengthen us every step of the way.

Throughout the book, you will find practical exercises, self-reflection prompts, and real-life stories of minority women who have succeeded in leadership roles. These tools and testimonies are designed to inspire, encourage, and equip you with the insights and strategies you need to thrive in your own leadership journey.

As we explore topics such as conducting a SWOT analysis on yourself, writing your "self-contract," and taking action steps to bring your vision to life, you will gain a deeper understanding of yourself and the unique gifts and talents God has bestowed upon you.

We will also delve into the importance of overcoming fear and embracing the fearless spirit that God has given us. By learning to trust in God's direction and seeking His guidance through prayer, scripture, and wise counsel, we can confidently step into our purpose and make a meaningful impact in our careers and communities.

Ultimately, this book is a testament to the power of faith, resilience, and the unshakable determination of minority women who refuse to be defined by societal limitations. It is a celebration of the God-given potential that resides within each of us and a rallying cry for us to rise up and embrace our divine purpose.

As you read through these pages, my prayer is that you will find encouragement, wisdom, and practical tools to help you navigate the challenges and triumphs of being a minority woman in leadership. May you discover the strength that lies within you, the faith that sustains you, and the purpose that propels you forward.

Remember, you are not alone on this journey. You are part of a sisterhood of resilient, faith-filled women who are breaking barriers, shattering stereotypes, and leaving a lasting impact on the world. Together, we will support, inspire, and empower one another as we pursue our God-given purpose with unwavering conviction.

So, let us step forward with courage, armed with the knowledge that our lives have been orchestrated by a loving God who has great plans for us. Let us embrace the challenges, celebrate the victories, and lean into the faith that will guide us every step of the way.

Welcome to "I need to be my authentic self!" May this book be a source of inspiration, encouragement, and practical wisdom as you embark on this transformative journey of faith, purpose, and leadership.

Get ready to unveil your dream, embrace your God-given identity, and step into the fullness of who you were created to be. The journey ahead is filled with possibilities, and I am honored to walk alongside you as we navigate this path together.

CHAPTER ONE

The Struggles Of Being A Minority Woman In Leadership

As I stepped into my first leadership role, I was filled with a mix of excitement and trepidation. I had worked tirelessly to earn this position, overcoming numerous obstacles and setbacks along the way. As a minority woman, I knew that the path ahead would be far from easy. The challenges I would face in management would test my resilience, determination, and faith like never before. Nevertheless I also knew deep in my soul that I was called to leadership for a reason....that my unique perspectives, skills, and passion for empowering others were needed now more than ever.

Growing up, I had always been driven by a deep sense of purpose. From a young age, my parents instilled in me the values of hard work, education, and service to others. As I progressed through school and entered the workforce, I began to realize that my desire to make a difference went beyond just excelling in my career. I felt a strong calling to use my talents and influence to create positive change and to open doors for other women and minorities who had traditionally been underrepresented in positions of power.

However, as I began to ascend the ranks of leadership, I quickly realized that the playing field needed to be higher. Despite my qualifications and track record of success, I found myself facing a barrage of microaggressions, stereotypes, and systemic barriers at every turn. In meetings, my ideas were often dismissed or overlooked in favor of those of my male colleagues. I was held to higher standards of performance and scrutinized more closely than my white male peers. Despite putting in long hours and consistently going above and beyond, I was passed over for promotions and high-profile assignments time and time again.

At first, I tried to brush off these experiences and focus on my work. I told myself that if I just kept my head down and proved my worth through my results, eventually my contributions would be recognized and rewarded. As the slights and setbacks continued to pile up, I found myself questioning my own abilities and worth. The constant pressure to outperform and overachieve just to be seen as "good enough" began to take a toll on my mental and emotional well-being. I felt like I was constantly walking on eggshells, trying to navigate the complex web of office politics and unspoken biases without losing my authenticity or compromising my values.

It was in these moments of self-doubt and frustration that I turned to my faith for guidance and strength. Through prayer and reflection, I was reminded that the opinions or actions of others did not define my worth and identity but my inherent dignity as a child of God. I leaned on the examples of strong, inspiring women in the Bible like Esther, Deborah, and Mary Magdalene, who had faced their own struggles and opposition but remained steadfast in their faith and purpose. I found solace in the words of Scripture, which promised that God had a plan and future for me and that no weapon formed against me would prosper.

Armed with this renewed sense of conviction, I began to approach the challenges of leadership with a different mindset. Rather than shrinking back or trying to blend in, I embraced my unique identity as a minority woman and used it as a source of strength and differentiation. I spoke up more assertively in meetings, even when it meant challenging the status quo or risking backlash. I sought out mentors and allies who could provide guidance and support, and I worked to build a network of other women and minority leaders who were facing similar struggles.

At the same time, I also recognized that simply excelling in my role was not enough to create lasting change. To truly break down the barriers and biases holding minority women back, I needed to use my platform and influence to advocate for systemic reforms and cultural shifts. I began to speak out more publicly about issues of diversity, equity, and inclusion and to challenge the deeply entrenched norms and power structures that perpetuated inequality in the workplace.

This was a challenging and uncomfortable path. There were many times when I felt like I was hitting my head against a brick wall or when the resistance and backlash I faced made me question whether it was all worth it. But in those moments, I drew strength from the progress and impact I could see slowly unfolding. As I mentored and sponsored other minority women and helped them to navigate the challenges of leadership, I saw glimpses of a brighter, more equitable future beginning to emerge. As I continued to use my voice and platform to drive change, I knew that every small victory was bringing us one step closer to a world where every woman, regardless of her race or background, could thrive and lead.

Looking back on those early years of my leadership journey, I am filled with both pride and humility. Pride in the resilience, courage, and determination that I and so many other minority women have shown in the face of daunting odds. Humility in the knowledge that our work is far from finished and that the fight for true equality and inclusion will require ongoing effort and sacrifice from us all.

However, I also feel a profound sense of hope and purpose. I know that every barrier we break down, every glass ceiling we shatter, and every door we open for the next generation of minority women leaders is a step towards a world where every person can fulfill their God-given potential and purpose. I believe with all my heart that this is the world we are called to create through our faith, our leadership, and our unwavering commitment to justice and equity.

So, to every minority woman who has ever felt the sting of discrimination or the weight of imposter syndrome, who has ever doubted her worth or questioned her place in the halls of power, I say this: You are not alone! Your struggles are real, and they are valid, but they do not define you! Your identity, your talents, and your purpose come from a higher source—from the God who created you in His image and who has a plan and future for you beyond anything you can imagine.

Navigating the Challenges of Being a Minority Woman in Management

Being a minority woman in a leadership position comes with its own unique set of challenges and obstacles. From the moment we step into a management role, we are confronted with a complex web of societal expectations, cultural biases, and systemic barriers that can make our path to success feel like an endless uphill climb.

One of the most pervasive and insidious challenges we face is the lack of representation and visibility of minority women in positions of power. Despite making up a significant portion of the overall workforce, women of color remain grossly underrepresented in top leadership roles across virtually every industry and sector. According to a recent study by McKinsey & Company, only 4% of C-suite executives in the

United States are women of color, compared to 68% who are white men. This lack of diversity at the highest levels of organizations sends a clear message about who is seen as valuable and capable of leadership. It creates a self-perpetuating cycle of exclusion and marginalization.

For those of us who do break through and ascend to management positions, the isolation and otherness we feel can be profound. We often find ourselves the only woman of color in the room, surrounded by a sea of faces that do not reflect our own experiences or perspectives. This lack of representation can lead to feelings of imposter syndrome, as we question whether we truly belong or have earned our place at the table. It can also make it difficult to build the kinds of relationships and networks that are essential for career advancement, as we may need help finding mentors, sponsors, or allies who understand and can relate to our unique challenges.

Moreover, as minority women in management, we often face a double bind of conflicting expectations and stereotypes based on our gender and race. On the one hand, we are expected to conform to traditional feminine norms of being nurturing, collaborative, and emotionally intelligent while also being assertive and decisive enough to be seen as strong leaders. On the other hand, we are also held to stereotypes and biases based on our race or ethnicity, which can paint us as angry, aggressive, or difficult to work with if we do not carefully modulate our tone and behavior.

Navigating these contradictory pressures can feel like walking a tightrope, where one misstep or moment of authentic expression can be quickly labeled as "unprofessional" or "not a good fit" for leadership. It requires a constant level of self-monitoring and code-switching that can be exhausting and demoralizing over time. It can make us feel like we are constantly performing rather than simply being ourselves.

In addition to these interpersonal challenges, minority women in management also face systemic barriers and inequities that can limit our opportunities for advancement and success. These can include everything from biased hiring and promotion practices to unequal pay and access to high-profile assignments to workplace cultures that are hostile or unwelcoming to diverse perspectives and experiences.

For example, research has consistently shown that women and minorities are held to higher standards of performance and competence than their white male counterparts and are more likely to be penalized for mistakes or missteps. We are also less likely to receive the kinds of challenging assignments, high-profile projects, or strategic roles that are essential for building our skills and visibility within an organization. Often times, when we do excel and achieve success, our accomplishments are often attributed to luck or affirmative action, rather than our own talents and hard work.

Minority women face significant barriers to career advancement, often lacking access to the informal networks and sponsorship systems that are crucial for success. In many organizations, leadership roles are filled through a "tap on the shoulder" process, where senior leaders identify and groom high-potential employees who resemble themselves. However, minority women may not have the same cultural or social capital as their white male counterparts, making it challenging to break into these inner circles.

This exclusion and marginalization create a self-reinforcing cycle where minority women are held back from advancing to higher levels of leadership, perpetuating the lack of diversity and representation at the top. Those who do break through often face immense pressure to constantly prove themselves and outperform their peers, which can take a toll on their mental and emotional well-being.

Despite these challenges, minority women have a unique and vital role to play in transforming leadership and driving positive change in organizations and communities. Their experiences navigating bias, exclusion, and adversity have equipped them with resilience, adaptability, and empathy – essential qualities for effective leadership in today's complex and rapidly changing world. The diverse perspectives and life experiences of minority women can bring fresh insights and innovative solutions, challenging the status quo and pushing organizations to be more inclusive, equitable, and responsive to the needs of all stakeholders.

As people of faith, minority women leaders have a higher calling and purpose that goes beyond personal success or advancement. They are called to use their talents and influence to serve others, be a voice for the voiceless, and work towards a more just and loving world. This means not only excelling in their leadership roles but also using their platforms to advocate for systemic change, mentor and empower other minority women, and create more inclusive and equitable cultures where everyone can thrive.

This path is challenging and uncomfortable, requiring boldness, courage, and persistence in the face of ongoing challenges and resistance. It means being willing to have difficult conversations, challenge entrenched power structures, and risk personal comfort and security for the sake of the greater good. However, this is the work that minority women of faith in leadership are called to do – to be a light in the darkness, a catalyst for transformation, and a testament to the power of diversity and inclusion. So, as we navigate the complex challenges of being minority women in management, let us draw strength from our faith, our sisterhood, and our shared purpose. Let us support and encourage one another, celebrate our victories, learn from our setbacks, and never lose sight of the bigger picture and higher calling that drives us. Let us trust that, with God's grace and guidance, we have everything we need to overcome any obstacle and achieve our fullest potential as leaders and changemakers.

Overcoming Stereotypes and Biases in the Workplace

As minority women in leadership, one of the most persistent and pernicious challenges we face is the prevalence of stereotypes and biases that seek to undermine our credibility, authority, and value in the workplace. These biases can take many forms, from overt discrimination and harassment to more subtle microaggressions and double standards that erode our confidence and limit our opportunities for advancement.

At the most basic level, minority women often face stereotypes and assumptions based on our race, ethnicity, and gender that paint us as less competent, less ambitious, or less leadership-material than our white male counterparts. These biases are deeply rooted in centuries of systemic oppression and marginalization. They are reinforced by media representations, cultural narratives, and societal norms that devalue the contributions and capabilities of women and people of color.

For example, Black women, in particular, often face the stereotype of the "angry black woman"—a trope that portrays us as overly aggressive, confrontational, and difficult to work with. This stereotype not only undermines our credibility and authority as leaders but also forces us to constantly monitor and modulate our tone and behavior to avoid being perceived as "threatening" or "unprofessional." Similarly, Asian women may face stereotypes of being passive, submissive, or lacking in leadership potential. In contrast, Latina women may be seen as overly emotional or "fiery" in ways that undermine their competence and professionalism.

These stereotypes and biases can manifest in a wide range of workplace interactions and experiences. We may face higher levels of scrutiny and criticism for our performance or decisions or have our ideas and contributions overlooked or dismissed in favor of those of our white male peers. We may be passed over for high-profile assignments or promotions or held to higher standards of accomplishment and competence than others in similar roles. We may face backlash or resistance when we assert ourselves or challenge the status quo, as our leadership is seen as a threat to existing power structures and hierarchies.

Moreover, minority women also face unique challenges at the intersection of race and gender that can compound the impacts of bias and discrimination. For example, we may be held to conflicting expectations around our appearance, communication style, and behavior that require us to constantly code-switch and adapt to different cultural norms and expectations. We may face pressure to downplay or minimize our racial or ethnic identity in order to be seen as more "professional" or "leadership material" while also being expected to take on additional emotional labor and diversity work that is not recognized or rewarded in the same way as other contributions.

The cumulative impact of these biases and challenges can take a heavy toll on our mental and emotional well-being as minority women in leadership. We may experience higher levels of stress, anxiety, and burnout as we navigate the constant pressure to prove ourselves and outperform our peers. We may struggle with imposter syndrome and self-doubt, questioning whether we truly belong or have earned our place at the table. We may face backlash or retaliation when we speak out about our experiences or advocate for change, as our voices are seen as disruptive or threatening to the status quo.

Despite these daunting challenges, I believe that minority women have the power and potential to overcome stereotypes and biases and thrive as leaders in the workplace. By developing a strong sense of self-awareness, resilience, and strategic savvy, we can navigate the complex landscape of bias and discrimination and emerge stronger and more effective on the other side.

One of the key strategies for overcoming bias and stereotypes is to cultivate a deep understanding of our unique strengths, talents, and experiences and to use them as a source of differentiation and value in the workplace. Rather than trying to fit into narrow molds or expectations of what a leader should look or act like, we can embrace our diversity as a strategic advantage and use it to bring fresh perspectives and innovative solutions to the table. This may require us to be more assertive in promoting our accomplishments and expertise, seeking out high-profile opportunities and stretch assignments, and building a strong personal brand and reputation that transcends stereotypes and assumptions.

Another crucial strategy is to build a robust network of mentors, sponsors, and allies who can provide guidance, support, and advocacy as we navigate the challenges of leadership. This may include seeking out other successful minority women leaders who can share their own experiences and strategies for overcoming bias, as well as cultivating relationships with influential allies across different levels and functions of the organization who can champion our work and help open doors to new opportunities. By surrounding ourselves with a diverse and supportive community, we can gain the confidence, resilience, and social capital needed to succeed in the face of adversity.

In addition to these individual strategies, minority women in leadership also have a vital role to play in driving systemic change and creating more inclusive and equitable workplace cultures. This may involve speaking out about our experiences and challenges and using our platforms and influence to raise awareness and advocate for policies and practices that promote diversity, equity, and inclusion. It may also involve mentoring and sponsoring other underrepresented groups and working to create more inclusive and welcoming environments where everyone can thrive and succeed.

Of course, driving this kind of change takes work and effort. It requires us to be courageous, persistent, and strategic in the face of ongoing resistance and backlash. It means being willing to have difficult conversations, challenge entrenched power structures and biases, and risk our comfort and security for the sake of the greater good. As minority women of faith in leadership, I believe that we are uniquely equipped and called to this work— to be a voice for the voiceless, a light in the darkness, and a catalyst for positive transformation in our workplaces and communities.

Ultimately, overcoming stereotypes and biases in the workplace is not just about our success or advancement as minority women leaders. It is about creating a more just, equitable, and loving world where everyone can thrive and reach their full potential, regardless of their race, gender, or background. It is about using our talents and influence to serve others, to be a force for good, and to help build the beloved community that God envisions for us all.

So, as we face the ongoing challenges and obstacles of bias and discrimination in the workplace, let us draw strength from our faith.

Real-Life Stories of Minority Women Who Have Succeeded in Leadership Roles

The stories of minority women who have defied the odds and achieved remarkable success in leadership roles serve as powerful testaments to the resilience, determination, and potential of women of color. These trailblazers have not only shattered glass ceilings and paved the way for future generations but have also made significant contributions to their industries and communities. By examining their journeys, we can gain valuable insights and inspiration for our leadership aspirations.

One such remarkable story is that of Rosalind Brewer, the current CEO of Walgreens Boots Alliance and the first African American woman to lead a Fortune 500 company. Brewer's journey to the top was challenging. She grew up in Detroit during the 1970s, a time when the city was grappling with economic instability and racial tensions. Despite these obstacles, Brewer excelled academically and earned a bachelor's degree in chemistry from Spelman College.

Brewer began her career as a scientist at Kimberly-Clark, where she quickly rose through the ranks, eventually becoming the company's first African American vice president. She later joined Walmart as a regional vice president. She made history in 2012 when she was appointed president and CEO of Sam's Club, becoming the first woman and first African American to lead a division of the retail giant.

Throughout her career, Brewer has been a vocal advocate for diversity and inclusion in the workplace. She has implemented initiatives to increase the representation of women and people of color in leadership roles and has been a mentor and sponsor to countless individuals. In her current role at Walgreens Boots Alliance, Brewer is leading the company through a transformative period, focusing on healthcare innovation, digitalization, and community engagement.

Brewer's success is a testament to her unwavering determination, strategic vision, and ability to break down barriers. She has faced numerous challenges and setbacks throughout her career but has always remained true to her values and purpose. In an interview with Forbes, Brewer shared her philosophy on leadership: "Leadership is about making others better as a result of your presence and making sure that impact lasts in your absence."

Another inspiring story is that of Sonia Syngal, the CEO of Gap Inc. and the first woman of color to lead the company. Syngal's journey is one of resilience and adaptability. Born in India, she immigrated to the United States with her family at the age of five and grew up in a small town in Pennsylvania. Syngal's parents instilled in her a strong work ethic and a belief in the power of education.

Syngal earned a bachelor's degree in mechanical engineering from Kettering University and a master's degree in manufacturing systems engineering from Stanford University. She began her career at Ford Motor Company, where she worked on improving manufacturing processes and reducing costs. In 2004, Syngal joined Gap Inc., as a Director of sourcing and quickly rose through the ranks, holding various leadership positions across the company's brands.

In 2020, Syngal was appointed CEO of Gap Inc., becoming the first woman and first person of color to lead the company in its 50-year history. Since taking the helm, Syngal has navigated the company through the challenges of the COVID-19 pandemic while also driving a strategic vision focused on digital transformation, sustainability, and inclusive design.

Syngal's leadership style is characterized by a deep commitment to empowering others and fostering a culture of inclusivity and belonging. In an interview with Fortune, she shared her approach to leadership: "I believe in the power of the team. I believe in the power of diversity of thought. I believe in the power of inclusion. And I believe in the power of creating an environment where people can bring their best selves to work."

Syngal's story is a powerful reminder that one's background or circumstances do not determine success but by the strength of one's character, the depth of one's vision, and the willingness to embrace change and challenge the status quo.

These are just two examples of the countless minority women who have achieved remarkable success in leadership roles. Other notable trailblazers include Mellody Hobson, co-CEO of Ariel Investments and chair of the board of Starbucks; Thasunda Brown Duckett, president and CEO of TIAA; and Lisa Su, president and CEO of Advanced Micro Devices (AMD).

Each of these women has faced unique challenges and obstacles on their path to leadership, but they have all demonstrated the resilience, determination, and vision necessary to succeed. They have not only broken barriers and shattered stereotypes but have also used their positions of influence to create more inclusive and equitable workplaces and communities.

As minority women in leadership, we can draw strength and inspiration from these stories. They serve as powerful reminders that success is possible, even in the face of significant adversity, and that our unique experiences and perspectives can be a source of strength and innovation in the workplace.

However, it is essential to recognize that these success stories do not negate the systemic barriers and biases that minority women continue to face in the workplace. While individual stories of triumph can inspire and motivate us, we must also work collectively to dismantle the structural inequities that limit opportunities for minority women in leadership.

This requires a commitment from individuals, organizations, and society as a whole to address issues of bias, discrimination, and lack of representation in the workplace. It involves creating inclusive cultures that value diversity, implementing policies and practices that promote equity, and providing mentorship and sponsorship opportunities for minority women at all levels of the organization.

As minority women in leadership, we have a unique role in driving these changes. By sharing our own stories and experiences, mentoring and sponsoring other minority women, and advocating for systemic change, we can help create a more equitable and inclusive future for all.

The path ahead may be challenging, but it is also filled with incredible potential and opportunity. By drawing strength from the stories of those who have come before us and by working together to create a more just and equitable world, we can ensure that every minority woman has the opportunity to thrive and lead with purpose and impact.

CHAPTER TWO

Cultural Barriers And The African American Experience

As an African American woman in leadership, I have often found myself navigating a complex landscape of cultural expectations, stereotypes, and systemic barriers. The journey has been one of both triumph and challenge, marked by moments of incredible pride in my heritage and moments of deep frustration with the obstacles that continue to limit opportunities for women who look like me.

Understanding the Unique Cultural Challenges Faced by African American Women

To fully understand the experiences of African American women in the workplace, we must first acknowledge the unique cultural challenges that shape our lives and careers. These challenges are rooted in a long history of oppression, discrimination, and marginalization that has created a legacy of economic, social, and educational disparities.

One of the most significant cultural challenges faced by African American women is the prevalence of negative stereotypes and controlling images that seek to limit our potential and define us in narrow, often demeaning ways. From the "angry black woman" trope to the "strong black woman" archetype, these stereotypes create a double bind that makes it difficult for African American women to navigate the workplace without facing judgment or backlash.

The "angry black woman" stereotype, in particular, has been a pervasive and damaging cultural narrative that paints African American women as aggressive, confrontational, and difficult to work with. This trope is often used to dismiss or discredit the legitimate concerns and experiences of African American women and to justify their exclusion from positions of power and influence.

At the same time, the "strong black woman" archetype, while ostensibly more positive, can also create unrealistic and burdensome expectations for African American women to be superhuman in their ability to handle stress, adversity, and the needs of others. This stereotype can lead to a lack of support and resources for African American women, as well as a reluctance to acknowledge or address the very real challenges and barriers they face in the workplace.

These stereotypes and cultural narratives are not just abstract concepts but have real and tangible impacts on the lives and careers of African American women. Research has shown that African American women are more likely to face discrimination, harassment, and bias in the workplace than their white counterparts and are often held to higher standards of performance and behavior.

For example, a study by the National Women's Law Center found that African American women are paid just 63 cents for every dollar paid to white, non-Hispanic men. This wage gap is even larger than the one faced by women overall. This disparity persists even when controlling for factors such as education, experience, and job title, suggesting that bias and discrimination play a significant role in limiting the economic opportunities of African American women.

Moreover, African American women are often excluded from the informal networks and systems of mentorship and sponsorship that can be critical for career advancement. In many organizations, leadership roles and opportunities are filled through a "tap on the shoulder" process, where high-potential employees are identified and groomed by senior leaders who see themselves reflected in their protégés. For African American women, who may not have the same cultural or social capital as their white counterparts, breaking into these inner circles can be an uphill battle.

These cultural challenges and barriers can take a heavy toll on the mental and emotional well-being of African American women in the workplace. The constant pressure to navigate bias, discrimination, and conflicting expectations can lead to higher levels of stress, anxiety, and burnout, as well as a sense of isolation and otherness that can be difficult to overcome.

Despite these challenges, I believe that African American women have a unique and vital role to play in transforming the cultural landscape of the workplace and driving positive change in our organizations and communities. Our experiences navigating adversity and marginalization have given us resilience, adaptability, and empathy, which are essential for effective leadership in today's complex and rapidly changing world. Our diverse perspectives and life experiences can bring fresh insights and innovative solutions to the table, challenging the status quo and pushing our organizations to be more inclusive, equitable, and responsive to the needs of all stakeholders.

Strategies for Breaking Through Cultural Barriers in Your Career

While the cultural barriers and challenges faced by African American women in the workplace are significant and systemic, there are strategies and approaches that we can use to navigate these obstacles and achieve new levels of success and influence in our careers.

One of the most important strategies is to develop a strong and positive sense of self rooted in a deep understanding and appreciation of our unique cultural heritage and identity. This means rejecting the negative stereotypes and controlling images that seek to limit or define us and instead embracing the richness, resilience, and creativity that have been the hallmarks of the African American experience.

It also means cultivating a healthy and authentic sense of self-esteem and self-worth, based not on external validation or achievement but on an inner knowing of our inherent value and dignity as human beings and children of God. When we are grounded in this sense of self, we are less likely to be swayed or discouraged by the biases and barriers we face and more likely to approach challenges with confidence, courage, and grace.

Another key strategy is to seek out and build a strong network of mentors, sponsors, and allies who can provide guidance, support, and advocacy as we navigate our careers. This may include seeking out other successful African American women leaders who can share their own experiences and strategies for breaking through cultural barriers, as well as cultivating relationships with influential allies across different levels and functions of the organization who can champion our work and help open doors to new opportunities.

Building these relationships requires a proactive and strategic approach, as well as a willingness to step outside of our comfort zones and engage with people who may be different from us in terms of race, gender, or background. It also requires a commitment to reciprocity and mutual support as we seek not only to benefit from the guidance and advocacy of others but also to pay it forward and create opportunities for those coming up behind us.

In addition to building a strong network, it is also important for African American women to develop a keen understanding of the unwritten rules and power dynamics that shape our organizations and industries. This means being attuned to the subtle cues and signals that can indicate bias or exclusion and being strategic in how we navigate and challenge these dynamics.

For example, we may need to be more assertive in promoting our accomplishments and expertise and in seeking out high-profile assignments and stretch opportunities that can help us build our skills and visibility. We may also need to be more vocal in calling out and challenging instances of bias or discrimination, even when doing so may be uncomfortable or risky.

At the same time, we must also be strategic in how we use our voice and influence and in choosing our battles wisely. This may mean picking our moments to speak up or push back and being intentional about framing our concerns or ideas in ways that are more likely to be heard and acted upon by those in positions of power.

Another important strategy for breaking through cultural barriers is to continually invest in our learning, growth, and development. This means seeking out opportunities to build new skills, gain new experiences, and expand our knowledge and expertise, both within and beyond our current roles and organizations.

It also means being open to feedback and constructive criticism and using it as an opportunity to learn and improve rather than as a personal attack or indictment of our worth. By cultivating a growth mindset and a commitment to lifelong learning, we can position ourselves to take on new challenges and opportunities and to adapt and thrive in the face of change and adversity.

Finally, breaking through cultural barriers requires a willingness to take risks and step outside of our comfort zones, even when doing so may be scary or uncomfortable. This may mean pursuing a new job or career path that aligns with our passions and values, even if it means leaving behind the security and familiarity of our current roles. It may mean starting our businesses or ventures and being willing to fail and learn from our mistakes along the way.

It may mean using our platforms and influence to speak out about the issues and injustices that matter most to us, even when doing so may be unpopular or controversial. By being willing to take bold and courageous action in pursuit of our goals and values, we can inspire others to do the same and create ripple effects of positive change that extend far beyond ourselves.

Celebrating the Strengths and Contributions of African American Women in the Workplace

While it is important to acknowledge and address the cultural barriers and challenges faced by African American women in the workplace, it is equally important to celebrate the incredible strengths, talents, and contributions that we bring to our organizations and communities.

African American women have a long and rich history of leadership, activism, and innovation in the face of adversity. From the trailblazing work of pioneers like Harriet Tubman and Sojourner Truth to the groundbreaking achievements of contemporary leaders like Michelle Obama and Kamala Harris, African American women have consistently challenged the status quo and pushed for social, political, and economic change.

In the workplace, African American women bring a wealth of unique perspectives, skills, and experiences that can drive innovation, creativity, and success. Our cultural background and lived experiences can provide valuable insights into diverse markets and communities, helping organizations to develop more inclusive and effective products, services, and strategies.

African American women are known for their strength, resilience, and determination in the face of adversity. We have a long history of persevering through challenges and setbacks and finding creative and resourceful ways to overcome obstacles and achieve our goals. This resilience and adaptability can be incredibly valuable in today's fast-paced and ever-changing business environment, where the ability to pivot and adjust to new circumstances is essential for success.

African American women are also known for their strong sense of community and social responsibility. Many of us have grown up with a deep understanding of the importance of giving back and paying it forward and of using our talents and resources to make a positive difference in the lives of others. This commitment to service and social impact can be a powerful asset in the workplace as organizations increasingly recognize the importance of corporate social responsibility and community engagement.

In addition to these strengths, African American women also bring a unique and valuable perspective to issues of diversity, equity, and inclusion in the workplace. Our experiences navigating bias, discrimination, and marginalization can provide valuable insights and strategies for creating more inclusive and equitable work environments and for driving systemic change at the organizational and societal levels.

By celebrating and leveraging African American women's strengths and contributions, organizations can tap into a powerful source of talent, innovation, and competitive advantage. Research has shown that companies with more diverse leadership teams and workforces tend to outperform their less diverse peers with higher levels of innovation, creativity, and financial performance.

Moreover, celebrating the achievements and contributions of African American women can help to challenge and dismantle the negative stereotypes and cultural barriers that have historically limited our opportunities and advancement. By highlighting the incredible successes and impact of African American women leaders, we can inspire and empower the next generation of young women to pursue their dreams and ambitions and to see themselves as capable and deserving of positions of power and influence.

Of course, truly celebrating the strengths and contributions of African American women in the workplace requires more than just lip service or token gestures. It requires a genuine commitment to creating a culture of inclusivity, equity, and belonging, where all employees feel valued, respected, and supported in bringing their full selves to work.

This means investing in the recruitment, retention, and advancement of African American women at all levels of the organization and providing the resources, opportunities, and support needed for them to thrive and succeed. It means actively seeking out and amplifying the voices and perspectives of African American women and ensuring that they are represented in key decision-making roles and processes.

It also means being willing to have honest and sometimes difficult conversations about race, bias, and privilege in the workplace and to take concrete actions to address and dismantle systemic barriers and inequities. This may require a willingness to challenge long-held assumptions and practices and invest in new approaches and initiatives that prioritize diversity, equity, and inclusion as core business imperatives.

Ultimately, celebrating the strengths and contributions of African American women in the workplace is not just a moral imperative but a strategic necessity for organizations that want to thrive and compete in an increasingly diverse and complex world. By tapping into the incredible talents, experiences, and perspectives of African American women, organizations can drive innovation, creativity, and success while also creating a more just, equitable, and inclusive society for all.

As African American women in leadership, we have a vital role to play in championing this vision and driving this change. Embracing our unique strengths and experiences and by using our platforms and influence to create more inclusive and equitable workplaces and communities, we can pave the way for a brighter and more just future for ourselves and for generations to come.

So, let us celebrate the incredible achievements and contributions of African American women in the workplace while also continuing to push for the systemic changes and cultural shifts needed to create true equity and inclusion for all. Let us lift each other, support each other's growth and success, and use our collective power to drive positive change and progress in our organizations and the world.

Let us never forget the incredible resilience, strength, and brilliance that lies within every one of us as African American women. For when we embrace and unleash our full potential, there is no limit to what we can achieve, and no barrier that we cannot overcome. We are the descendants of queens and warriors, of dreamers and trailblazers, and we have the power to shape the future and create a world where every woman, regardless of her race or background, can thrive and lead with purpose and impact.

CHAPTER THREE

Tapping Into Faith

As I reflect on my journey as a minority woman in leadership, I cannot overstate the profound impact that my Christian faith has had on my personal and professional growth. In the face of countless challenges and obstacles, it has been my unwavering faith in God that has sustained me, guided me, and empowered me to persevere and succeed.

How Faith Can Guide and Strengthen You in Your Career Journey

Faith is not just a source of comfort and inspiration; it is a powerful tool that can guide and strengthen us as we navigate the complexities and challenges of our career paths. When we anchor our lives in the unwavering truth of God's love and purpose for us, we gain a sense of clarity, resilience, and purpose that can propel us forward in the face of adversity.

One of the most significant ways that faith can guide us in our careers is by providing a clear sense of purpose and direction. As Christians, we believe that God has a unique plan and calling for each of our lives and that our work is an essential part of fulfilling that purpose. By seeking God's guidance and aligning our career goals with His will for our lives, we can find a deep sense of meaning and fulfillment in our work, even in the midst of difficult circumstances.

Faith provides a clear sense of purpose and direction, aligning our career goals with God's will for our lives.

Moreover, faith can provide us with the strength and resilience needed to overcome the many obstacles and setbacks that we may face in our careers. When we trust in God's sovereignty and goodness, we can find hope and courage in the face of disappointment, rejection, and failure. We can draw on the power of the Holy Spirit to persevere through challenges, knowing that God is with us and that He is working all things together for our good and His glory. Faith gives us strength and resilience to overcome obstacles and setbacks, drawing on the power of the Holy Spirit.

Faith can also help us to cultivate a sense of integrity, character, and values that can guide our decision-making and behavior in the workplace. As Christians, we are called to live out our faith in every aspect of our lives, including our professional endeavors. Aligning our actions and attitudes with biblical principles of honesty, compassion, and service, we can be a light and a witness to those around us and demonstrate the transformative power of faith in action.

Faith helps us to cultivate integrity, character, and values that can guide our decision-making and behavior in the workplace.

Biblical Principles for Success and Leadership

The Bible is a rich source of wisdom and guidance for every area of life, including our careers and leadership roles. By studying and applying biblical principles, we can develop a framework for success and effectiveness rooted in timeless truths and values.

One of the most fundamental biblical principles for success is the importance of hard work and diligence. Proverbs 13:4 tells us that "the soul of the sluggard craves and gets nothing, while the soul of the diligent is richly supplied." As leaders, we are called to model a strong work ethic, take responsibility for our tasks and commitments, and strive for excellence in all that we do.

The Bible emphasizes the importance of hard work and diligence as a key principle for success and effectiveness in leadership.

Another key biblical principle is the value of wisdom and discernment. Proverbs 4:7 urges us to "Get wisdom; get insight; do not forget, and do not turn away from the words of my mouth." As leaders, we must seek wisdom from God and wise counsel and use discernment to navigate complex situations and make sound decisions. This requires humility, openness to feedback, and a willingness to learn and grow.

The Bible highlights the value of wisdom and discernment in leadership, urging us to seek guidance from God and wise counsel.

The Bible also emphasizes the importance of servant leadership, a model of leadership that prioritizes the needs and well-being of others above personal gain or glory. Jesus himself embodied this principle, telling his disciples that "whoever would be great among you must be your servant" (Matthew 20:26). As leaders, we are called to use our influence and authority to serve and empower those we lead, to build up and encourage others, and to create a culture of collaboration and mutual respect.

Other biblical principles that can guide us in our leadership roles include:

- ❖ The importance of integrity and honesty.
- ❖ The value of forgiveness and grace.
- ❖ The power of prayer and dependence on God.

❖ The call to love and serve others as Christ loved us.

Developing a Strong Prayer Life and Relationship with God

At the heart of tapping into the power of faith in our career journeys is developing a deep and meaningful relationship with God through prayer and spiritual discipline. Prayer is the lifeline that connects us to God, by which we seek His guidance, wisdom, and strength in every aspect of our lives.

As leaders, we must prioritize our prayer lives and make time for regular communication with God. This may involve setting aside dedicated time each day for prayer and reflection, whether in the morning, during a break at work, or in the evening. It may also involve incorporating prayer into our daily routines and decision-making processes, seeking God's guidance and wisdom as we navigate the challenges and opportunities of our roles.

Developing a strong prayer life involves prioritizing regular communication with God and incorporating prayer into our daily routines and decision-making processes.

Developing a strong prayer life also requires cultivating a posture of humility, openness, and surrender to God's will. We must be willing to lay down our agendas and desires and trust in God's perfect plan and timing for our lives. We must also be open to hearing God's voice and responding to His promptings, even when they may challenge us or lead us in unexpected directions.

A strong prayer life requires a posture of humility, openness, and surrender to God's will, being willing to trust in His perfect plan and timing for our lives.

In addition to prayer, developing a strong relationship with God involves engaging in other spiritual disciplines such as Bible study, worship, and fellowship with other believers. By immersing ourselves in God's Word, we can gain wisdom, insight, and guidance for every area of our lives.

By worshiping and praising God, we can tangibly experience His presence and power. By connecting with other Christians in the community, we can find support, encouragement, and accountability as we seek to live out our faith in the workplace and beyond.

As we navigate the challenges and opportunities of leadership as minority women, let us remember that we are not alone. We have access to a power greater than ourselves, a God who loves us unconditionally and who has a perfect plan and purpose for our lives.

By tapping into the power of our Christian faith, we can find the guidance, strength, and wisdom we need to succeed and thrive in our careers and beyond. We can lead with integrity, compassion, and excellence and be a light and a witness to those around us.

Let us commit ourselves to prioritizing our relationship with God, to seeking His will and guidance in every aspect of our lives, and to living out our faith with boldness and authenticity. Let us trust in His goodness and sovereignty, even in the face of adversity and uncertainty.

As we do so, we will find that our faith is not just a source of comfort and inspiration but a powerful tool for transformation and impact. We will be empowered to break through barriers, shatter stereotypes, and achieve success on God's terms for His glory and the good of those we serve.

So, let us press on in faith, knowing that we are part of a greater story, a story of redemption, hope, and purpose. Let us anchor ourselves in the unshakable truth of God's love and grace, and let us step forward with courage and confidence, knowing that He who began a good work in us will carry it on to completion.

- ❖ Faith provides a clear sense of purpose and direction, aligning our career goals with God's will for our lives.

- ❖ Faith gives us strength and resilience to overcome obstacles and setbacks, drawing on the power of the Holy Spirit.

❖ Faith helps us to cultivate integrity, character, and values that can guide our decision-making and behavior in the workplace.

❖ The Bible emphasizes the importance of hard work and diligence as a key principle for success and effectiveness in leadership.

❖ The Bible highlights the value of wisdom and discernment in leadership, urging us to seek guidance from God and wise counsel.

❖ The Bible teaches the importance of servant leadership, prioritizing the needs and well-being of others above personal gain or glory.

❖ Developing a strong prayer life involves prioritizing regular communication with God and incorporating prayer into our daily routines and decision-making processes.

❖ A strong prayer life requires a posture of humility, openness, and surrender to God's will. We must be willing to trust in His perfect plan and timing for our lives.

❖ Developing a strong relationship with God involves engaging in spiritual disciplines such as Bible study, worship, and fellowship with other believers.

CHAPTER FOUR

Embracing God's Spirit

Fear is a powerful emotion that can hold us back from pursuing our dreams, taking risks, and stepping into the fullness of who God created us to be. As minority women in leadership, we often face unique fears and challenges that can make it difficult to navigate our career paths with confidence and courage. However, as Christians, we have access to a source of strength and boldness that can help us overcome even the most paralyzing fears. By embracing the truth that God did not give us a spirit of fear but of power, love, and a sound mind (2 Timothy 1:7), we can learn to step into our purpose with fearless faith and determination.

Understanding That God Did Not Give Us a Spirit of Fear (2 Timothy 1:7)

One of the most powerful truths in the Bible is found in 2 Timothy 1:7, where Paul writes, "For

God has not given us a spirit of fear, but of power and of love and of a sound mind." This verse reminds us that fear does not come from God; rather, it is a tool used by the enemy to keep us from fulfilling our God-given purpose and potential.

When we experience fear—whether it's fear of failure, rejection, or the unknown—we can easily fall into the trap of believing that we are not capable, qualified, or worthy of pursuing our dreams. These fears can manifest in various ways, such as self-doubt, anxiety, and insecurity, making it difficult for us to take the necessary steps forward in our careers and lives.

For minority women in leadership, these fears can be compounded by the unique challenges and obstacles we face in the workplace. We may fear that our voices will not be heard, that our contributions will not be valued, or that we will be judged or discriminated against because of our race or gender. These fears can be especially pronounced in environments where there is a lack of diversity or inclusive leadership, leading us to question our place and purpose in the organization.

Moreover, as Christians, we may also grapple with fears related to our faith and calling. We may fear that pursuing our career ambitions will lead us away from God's plan for our lives or that we will face persecution or rejection for expressing our beliefs in the workplace. These fears can create a sense of conflict or guilt, causing us to doubt our ability to integrate our faith and our work in a meaningful way.

However, the truth is that God has not given us a spirit of fear but of power, love, and a sound mind. When we truly embrace this truth, we can begin to see our fears in a different light—not as insurmountable obstacles but as opportunities for growth, faith, and reliance on God's strength.

The spirit of power that God has given us is not a power that comes from our abilities or achievements but from the same resurrection power that raised Christ from the dead (Ephesians 1:19-20). This power enables us to face challenges and overcome obstacles with courage and determination, knowing that we have the strength of the Holy Spirit within us. It gives us the boldness to speak up for what is right, to take risks for the sake of the gospel, and to pursue our God-given calling with confidence and conviction.

The spirit of love that God has given us is not based on our own merits or worthiness but on the unconditional love that God has for us as His beloved children. This love casts out fear (1 John 4:18) and enables us to extend grace, compassion, and empathy to others, even in the face of adversity or opposition. It gives us the capacity to build strong, authentic relationships and to create a sense of belonging and inclusivity in the workplace.

The spirit of a sound mind that God has given us is not a mind that is free from doubts or concerns but a mind that is anchored in the truth of God's Word and the wisdom of the Holy Spirit. This sound mind enables us to think clearly, make wise decisions, and discern God's will for our lives and careers. It gives us the ability to navigate complex challenges with creativity, adaptability, and resilience, trusting in God's guidance and provision every step of the way.

When we begin to embrace and walk in the spirit of power, love, and a sound mind that God has given us, we can start to break free from the chains of fear and step into our purpose with boldness and conviction. We can approach our careers and leadership roles not with timidity or uncertainty but with a deep sense of calling and a commitment to using our gifts and talents for God's glory and the good of others.

This does not mean that we will never experience fear or doubt again—as human beings, these emotions are a natural part of our journey. However, it does mean that we have a choice in how we respond to these emotions and in where we place our trust and confidence. By anchoring our lives in the unshakable truth of God's love and power, we can learn to face our fears with faith, knowing that He who is in us is greater than he who is in the world (1 John 4:4).

- ❖ Fear is not from God but a tool used by the enemy to keep us from our purpose and potential.

- ❖ Minority women in leadership face unique fears related to discrimination, lack of diversity, and integrating faith and work.

- ❖ God has given us a spirit of power, love, and a sound mind to overcome fear.

- ❖ The spirit of power enables us to face challenges with courage and determination.

- ❖ The spirit of love enables us to extend grace, compassion, and empathy to others.

- ❖ The spirit of a sound mind enables us to think clearly, make wise decisions, and discern God's will.

- ❖ Embracing and walking in the spirit of power, love, and a sound mind breaks the chains of fear.

❖ Anchoring our lives in God's love and power helps us face fears with faith.

Practical Ways to Overcome Fear and Step into Your Purpose

While embracing the biblical truth about fear is an essential first step, it's also crucial to develop practical strategies for overcoming fear in our daily lives and work. As minority women in leadership, we face unique challenges and obstacles that can make it easy to fall into patterns of fear and self-doubt. However, by implementing intentional practices and habits, we can learn to step into our purpose with courage, confidence, and faith.

✓ **Identify and confront your fears**: The first step in overcoming fear is to acknowledge its presence in your life. Take some time to reflect on the specific fears that are holding you back in your career and leadership journey. Write them down in a journal or share them with a trusted friend or mentor. Be honest with yourself about the thoughts, beliefs, and experiences that are fueling these fears and the impact they are having on your life and work.

Once you have identified your fears, the next step is to confront them head-on. This doesn't mean ignoring or suppressing them but rather facing them with intentionality and courage. Ask yourself, "What is the worst that could happen if I take this step or pursue this opportunity?" Often, when we examine our fears closely, we realize that the potential consequences are not as dire as we imagined and that we have the resilience and resources to handle whatever challenges may arise.

✓ **Reframe your perspective**: Fear often thrives on negative self-talk and limiting beliefs. As minority women in leadership, we may have internalized messages from society, family, or past experiences that tell us we are not good enough, smart enough, or capable enough to succeed. These messages can create a self-fulfilling prophecy, causing us to hold back from pursuing our goals and dreams out of fear of failure or rejection.

To overcome these limiting beliefs, we must learn to reframe our perspective and adopt a growth mindset. Instead of viewing challenges as threats or obstacles, we can choose to see them as opportunities for learning, growth, and innovation. Instead of defining ourselves by our failures or setbacks, we can choose to focus on our strengths, values, and unique contributions. One practical way to reframe your perspective is to practice gratitude and positive self-talk. Take time each day to reflect on the things you are thankful for, both in your personal and professional life. Celebrate your accomplishments and progress, no matter how small they may seem. When you catch yourself engaging in negative self-talk or self-doubt, interrupt those thoughts with affirmations and truths from God's Word.

✓ **Take action, even in the face of fear**: Fear often paralyzes us into inaction, causing us to put off important tasks, conversations, or decisions out of a sense of uncertainty or self-preservation. However, the only way to truly overcome fear is to take action in spite of it. This doesn't mean recklessly pursuing every opportunity or ignoring potential risks, but rather being willing to step outside your comfort zone and take calculated risks in pursuit of your goals and purpose.

One way to take action in the face of fear is to break down your goals into small, manageable steps. Instead of focusing on the result, which can feel overwhelming or impossible, focus on the next right step you can take today. This might mean sending an email, scheduling a meeting, or reaching out to a mentor for guidance. By taking consistent, intentional action, you build momentum and confidence and gradually chip away at the fears that once held you back.

Another way to take action is to surround yourself with a supportive community of mentors, peers, and accountability partners who can encourage and challenge you to step into your purpose. Seek out relationships with other minority women leaders who have overcome similar fears and challenges and can offer wisdom and guidance from their own experiences. Join professional organizations or affinity groups that provide opportunities for networking, skill-building, and advocacy.

✓ **Cultivate a daily practice of faith and surrender**: As Christian women in leadership, our ultimate source of strength and courage comes from our relationship with God. When we root our identity and purpose in Him, we can face any fear or challenge with the confidence that He is with us and for us and that His plans for us are good and perfect.

To cultivate a daily practice of faith and surrender:

- Start by setting aside dedicated time each day for prayer, Bible study, and reflection.

- Use this time to seek God's guidance and wisdom for your life and leadership and to align your thoughts and actions with His will and Word.

- Be honest with God about your fears and struggles, and invite Him to transform your mind and heart through the power of the Holy Spirit.

- Another way to cultivate faith and surrender is to practice letting go of control and trusting in God's sovereignty and timing. As leaders, it can be tempting to try to manage every outcome and detail, but ultimately, we must recognize that God is the one who holds the future in His hands. When we surrender our plans and desires to Him, we open ourselves up to His perfect will and purpose, even if it looks different from what we had imagined.

✓ **Redefine failure as a learning opportunity**: One of the biggest fears that holds us back as leaders is the fear of failure. We may worry about making mistakes, disappointing others, or damaging our reputation or career prospects. However, the truth is that failure is an inevitable part of the learning and growth process and can actually be a valuable source of insight and resilience.

To redefine failure as a learning opportunity:

- Start by shifting your mindset from a fixed to a growth perspective.

- Instead of viewing failure as a reflection of your worth or ability, view it as a chance to learn, adapt, and improve.

- When you experience a setback or disappointment, take time to reflect on what you can learn from the experience and how you can apply those lessons to future situations.

Another way to reframe failure is to celebrate your efforts and progress rather than just your outcomes. Recognize that success is not a straight line but a series of ups and downs, twists and turns. Every step you take towards your goals and purpose is a victory, regardless of the immediate results. By focusing on your growth and development rather than just your achievements, you build a sense of resilience and persistence that can carry you through any challenge or setback.

✓ **Practice self-care and self-compassion**: As minority women in leadership, we often face intense pressure to perform, achieve, and prove ourselves in a society that may not always value or recognize our contributions. This pressure can lead to burnout, stress, and a sense of inadequacy or imposter syndrome, which can fuel our fears and hold us back from stepping into our full potential.

To combat these pressures and maintain a sense of well-being and purpose, it's essential to prioritize self-care and self-compassion in your daily life and leadership. This means taking intentional steps to nurture your physical, emotional, and spiritual health, such as getting enough rest, exercise, and nutrition, setting boundaries around your time and energy, and engaging in activities that bring you joy and fulfillment.

Self-compassion also means treating yourself with kindness, understanding, and grace, even in the face of mistakes, failures, or challenges. Instead of beating yourself up or engaging in negative self-talk, practice speaking to yourself with the same compassion and encouragement you would offer to a dear friend or colleague. Recognize that you are human and that your achievements or perfection do not define your worth and value but your inherent dignity and beloved status as a child of God.

✓ **Keep your eyes on the bigger picture**: Finally, one of the most powerful ways to overcome fear and step into your purpose is to keep your eyes on the bigger picture of God's plan and purpose for your life and leadership. When we get caught up in the day-to-day challenges and pressures of our roles, it can be easy to lose sight of the ultimate reason why we do what we do and the impact we are called to make in the world.

To stay anchored in your purpose, take time regularly to reflect on your core values, passions, and calling. What are the unique gifts and experiences God has given you, and how can you use them to serve and empower others? What are the issues and causes that break your heart, and how can you use your leadership to make a positive difference in those areas? What is the legacy you want to leave behind, and how can you align your actions and decisions with that vision?

By keeping your eyes on the bigger picture, you can maintain a sense of perspective and purpose, even in the face of fears, challenges, and setbacks. You can trust that God is using every experience and circumstance to shape and refine you into the leader He has called you to be and that your faithfulness and obedience will bear fruit in His perfect timing and plan.

✓ Identify and confront your fears by reflecting on their root causes and impacts.

✓ Reframe your perspective by adopting a growth mindset and practicing gratitude and positive self-talk.

✓ Take action in the face of fear by breaking down goals into small steps and surrounding yourself with support.

✓ Cultivate a daily practice of faith and surrender through prayer, Bible study, and letting go of control.

✓ Redefine failure as a learning opportunity by shifting to a growth mindset and celebrating progress.

✓ Practice self-care and self-compassion by prioritizing your well-being and treating yourself with grace.

✓ Keep your eyes on the bigger picture of God's plan and purpose for your life and leadership.

The Role of Faith in Building Confidence and Courage

As minority women navigate the challenges and fears of leadership, it can be easy to feel overwhelmed, inadequate, or alone. However, the truth is that we have access to a source of strength, wisdom, and courage greater than ourselves, which can empower us to face any obstacle or opportunity with bold faith and determination. That source is our relationship with God and the unshakable confidence that comes from knowing who we are in Him.

Faith is the foundation upon which we build our identity, purpose, and leadership as Christian women. It is the lens through which we view ourselves, others, and the world around us and the anchor that keeps us steady and secure in the midst of life's storms and uncertainties. When we place our faith in God, we do not just believe in a set of abstract principles or doctrines but in a living, loving, and active presence that is intimately involved in every aspect of our lives and leadership.

One of the most powerful ways that faith builds our confidence and courage is by reminding us of our true identity and worth in Christ. As believers, we are not defined by our accomplishments, titles, or status but by our relationship with God and our position as His beloved children. We are created in His image, redeemed by His grace, and called to a purpose and destiny greater than anything we could achieve on our own.

This truth has profound implications for how we approach our leadership roles and responsibilities. Instead of striving for perfection or validation from others, we can rest in the assurance that we are already accepted, valued, and loved by God, regardless of our performance or outcomes. Instead of shrinking back from challenges or opportunities out of fear or self-doubt, we can step forward with boldness and courage, knowing that God is with us and for us and that He will equip and empower us for every good work He has prepared for us to do.

Another way that faith builds our confidence and courage is by giving us a sense of perspective and purpose that transcends our immediate circumstances and challenges. When we view our leadership through the lens of God's larger story and plan for the world, we can see that our roles and contributions are not just about advancing our agendas or interests but about participating in His redemptive work and advancing His kingdom on earth.

This perspective can be especially empowering for minority women in leadership, who may face unique obstacles and barriers in their careers and communities. When we anchor our identity and purpose in God, we can approach these challenges not as insurmountable obstacles but as opportunities to display His power, wisdom, and grace in our lives and leadership. We can trust that every struggle and setback is ultimately working together for our good and His glory and that He is using us to break down barriers, shatter stereotypes, and create new pathways for others to follow.

Faith also builds our confidence and courage by giving us access to a community of support, encouragement, and accountability that extends beyond our immediate circles and networks. As Christians, we are part of a global family of believers who share our values, struggles, and hopes and who can offer us guidance, mentorship, and prayer as we navigate the ups and downs of leadership. By connecting with other minority women leaders of faith, we can find solidarity, inspiration, and practical wisdom for how to thrive and make a difference in our unique contexts and callings.

Moreover, being part of a faith community can help us cultivate the spiritual disciplines and practices that are essential for maintaining our confidence, courage, and well-being as leaders. When we prioritize time for prayer, worship, Bible study, and fellowship with other believers, we are not just engaging in religious rituals or obligations, but in life-giving habits that renew our minds, strengthen our spirits, and deepen our relationship with God. These practices can help us stay grounded in our identity and purpose, even in the face of stress, pressure, or discouragement, and can provide us with the wisdom, discernment, and strength we need to lead with integrity, compassion, and excellence.

Finally, faith builds our confidence and courage by giving us a source of hope and resilience that can carry us through even the darkest and most difficult seasons of leadership. As minority women, we may face systemic barriers, personal challenges, and societal prejudices that can make us feel like giving up or giving in to despair. However, our faith reminds us that we are not alone in these struggles and that we have a God who is able to do immeasurably more than we could ask or imagine, according to His power at work within us (Ephesians 3:20).

CHAPTER FIVE

Conducting A SWOT Analysis On Yourself

As I've navigated my career journey as a minority woman in leadership, I've come to realize that self-awareness is one of the most powerful tools for personal and professional growth. When we take the time to deeply understand ourselves—our strengths, weaknesses, opportunities, and threats—we gain clarity and perspective that can guide us toward our goals and purpose with greater intention and effectiveness.

The Importance of Self-Awareness in Career Growth

Self-awareness is the foundation of personal and professional development. It's the ability to see ourselves clearly and objectively, to understand our thoughts, emotions, behaviors, and how they impact ourselves and others. When we cultivate self-awareness, we gain a deeper sense of who we are, what we want, and what we need to do to get there.

In the context of career growth, self-awareness is essential for several reasons:

- It helps us to identify our unique strengths and talents and how we can leverage them to add value and make a meaningful impact in our roles and organizations.

- It allows us to recognize our weaknesses and blind spots and to develop strategies for overcoming them or compensating for them through collaboration, delegation, or skill-building.

- It enables us to make more informed and intentional career choices based on our values, interests, and long-term goals rather than just external factors like salary or status.

- It empowers us to communicate our needs, boundaries, and expectations more effectively and to build more authentic and productive relationships with colleagues, mentors, and leaders.

- It gives us the resilience and adaptability to navigate change, uncertainty, and setbacks by keeping us grounded in our sense of self and purpose.

In my career journey, I've found that the more I've invested in my self-awareness, the more clarity, confidence, and direction I've had in my decision-making and leadership. It's not always been easy or comfortable to look at myself honestly and objectively, but it's been incredibly rewarding and transformative.

One key tool that has helped me cultivate self-awareness is the SWOT analysis, a framework for assessing both internal and external factors that impact our success and growth. By conducting a SWOT analysis on myself, I've gained valuable insights into my unique strengths, areas for improvement, opportunities for growth, and potential obstacles or threats to my progress.

In this chapter, I'll share my experience conducting a SWOT analysis on myself and how this simple yet powerful exercise has helped me identify my unique gifts and talents, overcome my limitations and blind spots, and create a roadmap for my career and life that aligns with my values, passions, and purpose.

How to Identify Your Strengths, Weaknesses, Opportunities, and Threats

The SWOT analysis is a tool that originated in the business world as a way for organizations to assess their internal and external environments and develop strategic plans for growth and success. However, the same principles can be applied to individuals looking to gain clarity and direction in their personal and professional lives.

SWOT stands for Strengths, Weaknesses, Opportunities, and Threats. By conducting a SWOT analysis on ourselves, we can gain a holistic and balanced view of our current situation and identify areas where we can leverage our strengths, address our weaknesses, seize opportunities, and mitigate threats.

Here's a step-by-step guide to conducting a SWOT analysis on yourself:

Identify Your Strengths

Start by reflecting on your unique strengths and talents—the things that come naturally to you, that you enjoy doing, and that you receive positive feedback on from others. Consider your skills, knowledge, experience, personality traits, and values that set you apart and add value to your work and relationships.

Some questions to ask yourself:

- What am I naturally good at?

- What do I enjoy doing, and what energizes me?

- What skills or expertise have I developed through my education, training, or experience?

- What personal qualities or character strengths do I possess?

- What do others often praise or appreciate about me?

Examples of strengths:

- Strong communication and interpersonal skills

- Creativity and innovation

- Analytical and problem-solving abilities

- Leadership and team-building

- Adaptability and resilience

- Empathy and emotional intelligence

- Technical expertise in a specific area

- Project management and organizational skills

As you identify your strengths, be specific and concrete. Instead of just listing "communication skills," for example, specify what kinds of communication you excel at, such as public speaking, written communication, or facilitating group discussions. The more specific you can be, the more actionable and valuable your insights will be.

Identify Your Weaknesses

Next, consider your weaknesses and areas for improvement—the things that you struggle with, that drain your energy, or that hold you back from reaching your full potential. Again, try to be honest and specific without being overly self-critical or judgmental.

Some questions to ask yourself:

- What tasks or activities do I tend to procrastinate or avoid?

- What skills or knowledge gaps do I have that limit my effectiveness?

- What personal habits or behaviors do I have that hinder my success?

- What feedback have I received from others about areas where I could improve?

- What are my blind spots or unconscious biases that may impact my decision-making or relationships?

Examples of weaknesses:

- Lack of experience or expertise in a particular area

- Difficulty with time management or prioritization

- Tendency to micromanage or have difficulty delegating

- Discomfort with public speaking or presenting

- Lack of assertiveness or confidence in certain situations

- Resistance to change or new ideas

- Difficulty with work-life balance or stress management

- Limited network or visibility within the organization

As with strengths, be specific and concrete when identifying your weaknesses. Instead of just saying "time management," for example, specify what aspects of time management you struggle with, such as prioritizing tasks, estimating how long tasks will take, or getting easily distracted.

It's important to note that weaknesses are not necessarily negative or shameful things. They are simply areas where we have room for growth and improvement. By acknowledging our weaknesses honestly and compassionately, we can develop strategies for addressing them and turning them into opportunities for learning and development.

Identify Your Opportunities

The next step is to look at the external opportunities that are available to you—the trends, changes, and possibilities in your industry, organization, or community that you can leverage to advance your goals and make a positive impact. Consider the relationships, resources, and experiences that you can pursue to learn, grow, and contribute.

Some questions to ask yourself:

- What trends or changes are happening in my industry or field that I could take advantage of?

- What new skills, technologies, or best practices are emerging that I could learn and apply?

- What projects, initiatives, or roles within my organization could I take on to expand my experience and visibility?

- What professional organizations, conferences, or networking events could I engage with to build my knowledge and connections?

- What mentors, sponsors, or collaborators could I seek out to support and guide my growth and development?

Examples of opportunities:

- Taking on a stretch assignment or leadership role within your current organization

- Pursuing a certification or advanced degree to build your expertise and credibility

- Joining a professional association or industry group to expand your network and knowledge

- Attending a conference or workshop to learn about emerging trends and best practices

- Collaborating with colleagues from different departments or functions to drive innovation and change

- Seeking out a mentor or sponsor who can provide guidance and advocacy for your career advancement

- Exploring new career paths or industries that align with your strengths and passions

As you identify opportunities, think broadly and creatively. Don't limit yourself to the obvious or immediate options; consider the long-term possibilities and the potential impact you could make. Also, be strategic in pursuing opportunities that align with your strengths, values, and goals rather than just chasing every shiny object that comes your way.

Identify Your Threats

Finally, consider the external threats and challenges that you face—the obstacles, risks, and limitations that could derail your progress or compromise your success. Think about the competitive landscape, the economic and political climate, and the social and cultural barriers that you may encounter as a minority woman in leadership.

Some questions to ask yourself:

- What are the biggest challenges or obstacles in my industry or organization that could impact my career growth?

- What are the potential risks or downsides of pursuing certain opportunities or making certain career moves?

- What are the cultural or systemic barriers that I may face as a minority woman in my field or organization?

- What are the competitive pressures or market changes that could impact my job security or advancement prospects?

- What are the personal or family obligations that could limit my ability to take on new roles or responsibilities?

Examples of threats:

- Lack of diversity and inclusion in your industry or organization, leading to bias and discrimination

- Economic downturns or budget cuts that could impact your job security or advancement opportunities

- Rapidly changing technologies or market conditions that could make your skills or expertise obsolete

- Competitive pressures from other candidates or colleagues vying for the same roles or opportunities

- Cultural or societal barriers, such as stereotypes or double standards, could limit your credibility or influence

- Personal or family challenges, such as health issues or caregiving responsibilities, could impact your ability to perform or advance in your career

As with the other components of the SWOT analysis, be specific and realistic when identifying threats. Don't let fear or pessimism cloud your judgment, but also don't ignore potential risks or challenges that could impact your success. The goal is to have a clear and accurate picture of the external factors that could influence your career so that you can develop strategies for navigating them effectively.

- The SWOT analysis is a framework for assessing both our internal and external factors that impact our success and growth by identifying our Strengths, Weaknesses, Opportunities, and Threats.

- To conduct a SWOT analysis on yourself, start by reflecting on your strengths and talents and be specific and concrete in identifying them.

- Next, honestly and compassionately consider your weaknesses and areas for improvement and develop strategies for addressing them and turning them into opportunities for growth.

- Look for external opportunities that align with your strengths, values, and goals and that allow you to make a positive impact and advance your career.

- Finally, identify the external threats and challenges that you may face and develop strategies for navigating them effectively without letting fear or pessimism hold you back.

Using Your SWOT Analysis to Create a Personal Development Plan

Conducting a SWOT analysis is a powerful exercise in self-reflection and self-awareness, but the real value comes from translating those insights into action. Once you've identified your strengths, weaknesses, opportunities, and threats, the next step is to use that information to create a personal development plan that outlines specific goals, strategies, and actions for your growth and success.

A personal development plan is a roadmap for your career and life that helps you clarify your vision, set measurable goals, and identify the steps and resources you need to achieve them. It's a living document that you can revisit and revise regularly as your circumstances and priorities change and as you gain new insights and experiences along the way.

Here are some key elements to include in your personal development plan:

- **Vision and values statement**: Start by articulating your long-term vision for your career and life—the impact you want to make, the legacy you want to leave, and the values and principles that guide your choices and actions. This serves as a north star for your personal and professional development and helps you stay focused and aligned with your purpose even in the face of challenges or distractions.

- **SMART goals**: Next, identify specific, measurable, achievable, relevant, and time-bound (SMART) goals that align with your vision and values, and that leverage your strengths and opportunities while addressing your weaknesses and threats. Break down larger, long-term goals into smaller, short-term objectives that you can work towards incrementally.

Examples of SMART goals:

- Develop and deliver a keynote presentation on diversity and inclusion in tech at a major industry conference within the next six months.

- Complete a project management certification course and apply the skills to lead a cross-functional initiative within my organization by the end of the year.

- I aim to build and maintain relationships with at least three senior leaders in my organization who can serve as mentors and sponsors for my career growth over the next 12 months.

- **Action steps and resources**: For each goal, identify the specific actions and resources you need to achieve it. These could include taking courses or workshops, seeking out mentors or coaches, joining professional organizations or networks, or practicing new skills and behaviors in your daily work and interactions. Be specific and realistic in your action steps, and break them down into manageable tasks that you can schedule and track.

- **Metrics and milestones**: Establish clear metrics and milestones for tracking your progress and celebrating your achievements along the way. This could include quantitative measures like the number of new skills or certifications you acquire or qualitative measures like feedback from colleagues or mentors on your growth and impact. Regularly review and update your plan based on your progress and any new insights or opportunities that arise.

- **Accountability and support**: Finally, identify the people and resources that can hold you accountable and support you in your development journey. This could include a mentor or coach who can provide guidance and feedback, a peer accountability partner who can help you stay on track and motivated, or a professional development budget or program within your organization that can fund your growth and learning. Be proactive in seeking out and leveraging these resources and in communicating your goals and progress to others who can champion and support you.

As you create your development plan, keep in mind that it's not a fixed or static document but a dynamic and evolving one that should reflect your ongoing growth and learning. Regularly revisit and update your plan based on new insights, experiences, and priorities, and be open to pivoting or adjusting your goals and strategies as needed.

Also, remember that personal and professional development is not a solo journey but a collaborative and interactive one that involves engaging with others and seeking out diverse perspectives and feedback. Feel free to share your plan with trusted mentors, colleagues, or friends who can offer guidance and support, and be open to learning from their experiences and insights as well.

Ultimately, creating a personal development plan based on your SWOT analysis is a powerful way to take ownership of your career and life and to proactively shape your own growth and success. By leveraging your unique strengths and opportunities and addressing your weaknesses and threats with intention and strategy, you can create an authentic, meaningful, and impactful roadmap for your development.

- A personal development plan is a roadmap for your career and life that helps you clarify your vision, set measurable goals, and identify the steps and resources you need to achieve them.

- Key elements of a personal development plan include a vision and values statement, SMART goals, action steps and resources, metrics and milestones, and accountability and support.

- Regularly revisit and update your personal development plan based on new insights, experiences, and priorities, and be open to pivoting or adjusting your goals and strategies as needed.

- Personal and professional development is a collaborative and interactive journey that involves engaging with others and seeking out diverse perspectives and feedback.

- Creating a personal development plan based on your SWOT analysis is a powerful way to take ownership of your career and life and proactively shape your growth and success.

In conclusion, conducting a SWOT analysis on yourself and using those insights to create a personal development plan is a transformative practice that can help you gain clarity, confidence, and direction in your career and life. By taking the time to deeply understand your unique strengths, weaknesses, opportunities, and threats and by proactively shaping your own growth and development, you can create an authentic, meaningful, and impactful roadmap for success.

As minority women in leadership, we face unique challenges and barriers in our career journeys. However, we also have incredible strengths, talents, and opportunities to make a positive difference in the world. By cultivating self-awareness, setting intentional goals, and leveraging our diverse experiences and perspectives, we can break through barriers, shatter stereotypes, and create new pathways for ourselves and those who come after us.

However, personal and professional development is not a one-time achievement or destination. It's an ongoing journey of growth, learning, and transformation that requires a commitment to continuous reflection, experimentation, and improvement. It's a collaborative and interactive process that involves seeking out diverse perspectives, feedback, and support from others who can challenge and encourage us along the way.

Ultimately, conducting a SWOT analysis and creating a personal development plan is not just about achieving external markers of success or achievement. It's about aligning our lives and leadership with our deepest values, passions, and purpose and about using our unique gifts and experiences to make a positive impact in the world.

As we navigate the ups and downs of our career journeys, may we remember that we are not alone but part of a powerful sisterhood of leaders who are breaking barriers, creating change, and paving the way for a more just and equitable world. May we draw strength and inspiration from each other's stories and successes, and may we continue to grow, learn, and transform together as we pursue our highest potential and purpose

CHAPTER SIX

Writing Your "Self-Contract"

As I've grown in my career and leadership journey, I've come to recognize the power of setting clear intentions, goals, and commitments for myself. It's not enough to simply react to the demands and expectations of others or to let my career path be determined by chance or circumstance. To truly thrive and fulfill my God-given purpose, I needed to take ownership of my own growth and development and hold myself accountable to the vision and values that guide me.

One of the most effective tools I've found for doing this is writing a "self-contract"—a personal document that outlines my goals, commitments, and action steps for my career and life. A self-contract is more than just a to-do list or a set of resolutions. It's a sacred covenant with myself, a promise to honor my own needs, desires, and potential and to align my actions with my deepest beliefs and values.

In this chapter, I'll share my experience writing my self-contract and how this practice has helped me stay focused, motivated, and accountable for my growth and success. I'll also offer some practical guidance and reflection questions to help you create your own self-contract and use it as a tool for personal and professional transformation.

Setting Goals and Commitments to Yourself and Your Career

The first step in writing a self-contract is to get clear on your own goals and commitments for your career and life. This requires a deep level of self-awareness and honesty, as well as a willingness to dream big and challenge yourself to grow beyond your current limitations.

Here are some of the key areas to consider when setting your goals and commitments:

- **Your values and priorities**: What matters most to you in your career and life? What are the non-negotiable principles and beliefs that guide your decisions and actions? For me, some of my core values include integrity, service, growth, and faith.

- **Your strengths and talents**: What are the unique gifts and abilities that you bring to your work and relationships? How can you leverage these strengths to make a positive impact and achieve your goals? For example, I know that I have a natural ability to connect with and inspire others, and I've used this strength to build strong teams and partnerships in my leadership roles.

- **Your passion and purpose**: What are the issues, causes, or problems that ignite your passion and sense of purpose? How can you align your career and life choices with these deeper callings? For me, my passion is to empower and uplift other minority women in leadership and to create more diverse, equitable, and inclusive workplaces and communities.

- **Your growth and development**: What are the skills, knowledge, and experiences that you need to acquire or strengthen in order to achieve your goals and fulfill your potential? What are the habits, mindsets, or behaviors that you need to cultivate or let go of? For example, I've committed to developing my public speaking and thought leadership skills and overcoming my tendency to overwork and neglect my self-care.

- **Your relationships and support**: Who are the people and communities that can support, challenge, and inspire you in your growth and success? How can you build and nurture these relationships in a mutually beneficial way? For me, this includes seeking out mentors and sponsors who can provide guidance and advocacy, as well as investing in my team and colleagues to create a culture of trust, collaboration, and growth.

Once you've reflected on these areas, it's time to translate them into specific, measurable, and time-bound goals and commitments. Here are some examples of goals and commitments that I've included in my self-contract:

- I commit to spending at least 30 minutes each day in prayer and scripture study, deepening my relationship with God and seeking His guidance for my life and work.

- I will develop and deliver at least one keynote speech or workshop per quarter to share my expertise and inspire others in my field.

- I will build and lead a diverse and inclusive team with at least 50% representation of women and people of color in leadership roles within the next two years.

- I will invest in my own self-care and well-being by taking at least one day off per week for rest and renewal and prioritizing my physical, mental, and emotional health.

- I will seek out and cultivate at least one new mentor or sponsor relationship each year to gain new perspectives and opportunities for growth and advancement.

Aligning Your Self-Contract with God's Purpose for Your Life

As a Christian leader, I believe that my ultimate purpose and fulfillment come from aligning my goals and actions with God's will and plan for my life. My self-contract is not just a personal document but a spiritual one—a way of discerning and embracing the unique calling and destiny that God has for me.

One key way that I align my self-contract with God's purpose is through prayer and scripture study. By spending time each day in quiet reflection and listening, I open myself up to the guidance and wisdom of the Holy Spirit. I ask God to reveal His vision and purpose for my life and to give me the courage and strength to follow it, even when it may be difficult or unconventional.

Another way that I align my self-contract with God's purpose is by seeking out godly counsel and community. I have a trusted circle of mentors, pastors, and friends who share my faith and values and who can offer wise and honest feedback on my goals and choices. I also make it a priority to serve and contribute to my church and faith community as a way of living out my calling and making a positive impact in the world.

Here are some reflection questions that I use to help align my self-contract with God's purpose:

- What are the unique gifts, talents, and experiences that God has given me, and how can I use them to serve and glorify Him?

- What are the needs, problems, or opportunities in the world that break my heart or ignite my passion, and how can I respond to them in a way that reflects God's love and justice?

- What are the biblical principles and values that should guide my career and life choices, and how can I apply them in a practical and relevant way?

- How can I cultivate a deeper relationship with God and seek His guidance and wisdom in every area of my life and work?

- How can I build and nurture a community of faith and support and use my influence and resources to make a positive impact in the world?

By regularly reflecting on these questions and seeking to align my self-contract with God's purpose, I find a deeper sense of meaning, fulfillment, and impact in my career and life. I know that I'm not just working for my own success or achievement but for a higher calling and a greater good.

Holding Yourself Accountable to Your Self-Contract

Writing a self-contract is one thing, but actually living it out is another. It's easy to get caught up in the day-to-day demands and distractions of work and life and to lose sight of our own goals and commitments. That's why it's so important to build accountability and support systems to help us stay on track and make progress towards our vision.

One key way that I hold myself accountable to my self-contract is by regularly reviewing and updating it. I set aside time each quarter to reflect on my progress, celebrate my successes, and identify areas for improvement or adjustment. I also share my self-contract with a trusted accountability partner, who can offer encouragement, feedback, and challenge when needed.

Another way that I hold myself accountable is by breaking down my larger goals into smaller, actionable steps and by tracking my progress along the way. For example, if one of my goals is to develop my public speaking skills, I might set a target of giving one presentation per month and then track my preparation, delivery, and feedback for each one. By celebrating the small wins and learning from the challenges, I build momentum and confidence towards my larger vision.

I also find it helpful to create visual reminders and cues of my self-contract to keep it front and center in my daily life. This might include posting my goals and commitments in a visible place, like my office or home, or creating a vision board or journal that captures my aspirations and inspiration. By surrounding myself with positive and purposeful messages, I reinforce my motivation and commitment to growth.

Finally, I hold myself accountable by being willing to course-correct and adapt when needed. I recognize that my self-contract is not a rigid or static document but a living and evolving one. As I gain new insights, experiences, or challenges, I may need to revise or refine my goals and commitments to stay aligned with my values and purpose. By embracing flexibility and learning, I can stay responsive and resilient in the face of change and uncertainty.

- A self-contract is a personal document that outlines your goals, commitments, and action steps for your career and life based on your values, strengths, passions, growth, and relationships.

- To create a self-contract, reflect on what matters most to you, what you're good at, what ignites your passion and purpose, what you need to learn and develop, and who can support and inspire you.

- Translate your reflections into specific, measurable, and time-bound goals and commitments, and break them down into smaller, actionable steps.

- Align your self-contract with God's purpose for your life by seeking His guidance through prayer and scripture, seeking godly counsel and community, and reflecting on how you can use your gifts and influence for His glory and the greater good.

- Hold yourself accountable to your self-contract by regularly reviewing and updating it, tracking your progress, creating visual reminders, and being willing to course-correct and adapt as needed.

Creating and living out a self-contract has been one of the most transformative practices in my leadership and life journey. It has helped me gain clarity, confidence, and conviction in my purpose and potential and stay focused and accountable for my growth and success.

But more than that, it has helped me to align my career and life with a deeper sense of meaning and mission. By seeking to discern and embrace God's purpose for my life and by using my gifts and influence to make a positive impact in the world, I find a profound sense of joy, fulfillment, and significance that goes beyond just achieving my own goals or advancing my career.

I believe that each of us has a unique and sacred calling, a divine purpose that we were created and equipped to fulfill. But it's up to us to discover and embrace that purpose and to take ownership of our growth and development in pursuing it.

Writing a self-contract is a powerful way to do just that. It's a way of claiming our own agency and authority, taking responsibility for our own choices and actions, and holding ourselves accountable to the vision and values that guide us.

It's also a way of surrendering to a higher power and purpose, of seeking to align our will with God's will, and of trusting in His guidance and provision as we navigate the ups and downs of our career and life journey.

As you create your self-contract, I encourage you to approach it with a spirit of curiosity, courage, and faith. Be willing to dream big, challenge yourself, and step outside of your comfort zone. But also, be willing to listen deeply, seek wisdom and guidance from others, and trust in the still, small voice of God that speaks to your heart and soul.

Remember that your self-contract is not just a personal document but a spiritual one. It's a way of honoring the sacred gift of your life and using it to make a positive difference in the world. It's a way of living out your faith in action and being a light and a witness to the love, grace, and power of God.

As you hold yourself accountable to your self-contract, be patient and compassionate with yourself. Recognize that growth and change take time and that setbacks and challenges are a natural part of the journey. But also celebrate your progress and successes, no matter how small or incremental they may seem.

And above all, trust in the goodness and faithfulness of God, who has begun a good work in you and will carry it to completion. Lean into His strength and wisdom, and let Him guide and sustain you every step of the way.

As a minority woman in leadership, you have a unique and valuable perspective to offer, a voice and a vision that the world needs to hear. By writing and living out your self-contract, you are claiming your place at the table and using your gifts and influence to create a more just, equitable, and thriving world for all.

So, my sisters, let us rise and embrace our sacred calling, our divine purpose, with courage, conviction, and faith. Let us write and live out our self-contracts with intention, integrity, and impact. Let us support and inspire one another along the way as we seek to be the change we wish to see in the world and to lead with love, grace, and purpose.

CHAPTER SEVEN

God's Direction In Your Career Path

As I've navigated the twists and turns of my career journey as a minority woman in leadership, I've come to realize that one of the most powerful and transformative aspects of my faith has been learning to trust in God's direction and guidance over my path and purpose.

It's easy to think that our careers are solely a product of our efforts, skills, and decisions. We may believe that we are the ones in control and that our success or failure rests entirely on our shoulders. But as Christians, we know that there is a higher power at work in our lives—a God who loves us, created us, and has a unique plan and purpose for each of us.

The book of Proverbs powerfully reminds us of this truth: "In their hearts, humans plan their course, but the Lord establishes their steps" (Proverbs 16:9, NIV). This verse suggests that while we may have our ideas and plans for our careers, it is ultimately God who directs and guides our path, often in ways that we could never have predicted or imagined.

So, what does it actually mean to trust in God's direction for our careers? How can we discern His will and guidance in the midst of the many choices, challenges, and opportunities that we face? And what does it look like to align our plans and purposes with His?

In this chapter, we'll explore these questions and more and discover how seeking and following God's direction in our career paths can lead to greater fulfillment, impact, and alignment with His purposes for our lives.

Trusting That God Directs Your Steps and Purpose (Proverbs 16:9)

The first step in opening ourselves up to God's direction in our careers is cultivating a deep trust and faith in His sovereignty and goodness. This means letting go of our own need for control and certainty and recognizing that God's ways are often beyond our understanding or expectations.

One of the most powerful examples of this kind of trust can be found in the story of Abraham, who God called to leave his homeland and family and go to a new land that God would show him (Genesis 12:1). Abraham had no idea where he was going or what God had in store for him. Still, he stepped out in faith, trusting that God's plan was better than his own.

Similarly, as we navigate our career journeys, we may face moments of uncertainty, confusion, or even fear. We may feel like we are walking in the dark, wondering which path to take or which opportunities to pursue. But it is in these moments that we have the opportunity to lean into our faith and trust that God is guiding our steps, even when we cannot see the way.

This kind of trust requires a fundamental shift in our mindset and perspective. Instead of seeing our careers as a ladder to climb or a series of accomplishments to achieve, we begin to see them as a journey of faith and obedience, a way of using our gifts and talents to serve God and others.

It also requires a willingness to surrender our plans and agendas and to be open to the unexpected detours and diversions that God may bring our way. We may have our hearts set on a particular job, promotion, or career path, but God may have a different plan in mind—one that challenges us, stretches us, and ultimately leads us to a greater sense of purpose and fulfillment.

Trusting in God's direction doesn't mean sitting back and doing nothing, waiting for Him to magically open doors or make decisions for us. Rather, it means actively seeking His guidance and wisdom and then stepping out in faith to follow where He leads.

Here are a few key strategies that have helped me and others:

❖ **Pray consistently and fervently**: One of the most powerful ways to discern God's will for our careers is through prayer. This means setting aside regular time to communicate with God, to share our hopes, fears, and desires, and to listen for His voice and direction. It means praying not just for specific outcomes or opportunities but for wisdom, discernment, and clarity in our decision-making. And it means trusting that God hears our prayers and is working behind the scenes to guide and direct our path, even when we cannot see it.

❖ **Study and meditate on Scripture**: Another key way to seek God's guidance is through His Word. The Bible is full of wisdom, guidance, and inspiration for every area of our lives, including our careers. By regularly reading, studying, and meditating on Scripture, we can gain a deeper understanding of God's character, purposes, and plans for our lives. We can find encouragement and direction in the stories of biblical figures who stepped out in faith and obedience, and we can apply the principles and promises of God's Word to our own career decisions and challenges.

❖ **Seek wise counsel from trusted mentors and advisors**: God often speaks to us through the wisdom and guidance of others, particularly those who are further along in their faith and career journeys. By seeking out mentors, advisors, and accountability partners who share our values and can offer godly perspectives and advice, we can gain valuable insight and direction for our career paths. This might include pastors, coaches, colleagues, or even friends and family members who can pray with us, listen to our concerns, and offer wisdom and encouragement.

❖ **Pay attention to your passions, gifts, and opportunities**: God has given each of us unique talents, interests, and experiences that can serve as clues to His purposes and plans for our lives. By paying attention to the things that bring us joy, energy, and a sense of meaning and impact, we can start to discern the areas where God may be calling us to invest our time and talents. We can also look for opportunities and open doors that align with our passions and skills and that allow us to use our gifts to serve others and make a difference in the world.

❖ **Be open to God's surprising and unconventional plans**: Sometimes, God's direction for our careers may not look like what we expected or planned. He may call us to take risks, make sacrifices, or pursue paths that seem unconventional or even foolish by the world's standards. But when we trust in His sovereignty and goodness, we can step out in faith, knowing that His plans are ultimately for our good and His glory. This might mean being open to unexpected job offers, career changes, or even moving to new cities or countries if that is where God is leading us.

Seeking and following God's guidance in our career decisions is not a one-time event but an ongoing journey of faith and obedience. It requires a posture of humility, receptivity, and willingness to follow where He leads, even when the path is unclear or uncomfortable.

Discerning God's Will Through Prayer, Scripture, and Wise Counsel

One of the most common questions that Christians face when it comes to career decisions is, "How can I know for sure that this is God's will for my life?" The desire to discern and follow God's perfect plan can feel overwhelming, especially when we are faced with multiple options or uncertain outcomes.

The good news is that God is not trying to hide His will from us or make it difficult to discern. Rather, He desires to guide and direct us and has given us tools and resources to help us understand and follow His leading.

The first and most important tool for discerning God's will is prayer. As we saw in the previous section, consistent and fervent prayer is essential for seeking God's guidance and wisdom in our career decisions. But prayer is not just about asking God for what we want or need; it's about aligning our hearts and minds with His and being open to His direction and correction.

One helpful way to pray for discernment is to use the ACTS model:

- ❖ **Adoration**: Begin by praising God for who He is and what He has done and acknowledging His sovereignty and goodness in your life.

- ❖ **Confession**: Next, confess any sins, doubts, or fears that may be hindering your ability to hear and follow God's voice, and ask for His forgiveness and cleansing.

- ❖ **Thanksgiving**: Then, give thanks for the blessings and opportunities that God has already provided in your career journey and for the ways He has guided and protected you thus far.

❖ **Supplication**: Finally, bring your specific career decisions and concerns before God and ask for His wisdom, clarity, and direction. Be open to His leading, even if it differs from your plans or preferences.

In addition to prayer, scripture is another powerful tool for discerning God's will. The Bible is full of principles, promises, and examples that can guide and inspire us in our career decisions. Some key passages to study and meditate on include:

❖ Proverbs 3:5-6: "Trust in the Lord with all your heart and lean not on your own understanding; in all your ways submit to him, and he will make your paths straight."

❖ Jeremiah 29:11: "'For I know the plans I have for you,' declares the Lord, 'plans to prosper you and not to harm you, plans to give you hope and a future.'"

❖ Romans 12:1-2: "Therefore, I urge you, brothers and sisters, in view of God's mercy, to offer your bodies as a living sacrifice, holy and pleasing to God—this is your true and proper worship. Do not conform to the pattern of this world, but be transformed by the renewing of your mind. Then you will be able to test and approve what God's will is— his good, pleasing and perfect will."

As we study and apply these and other scriptures to our career decisions, we can begin to develop a biblical framework for understanding God's purposes and plans for our lives.

Finally, seeking wise counsel from trusted mentors, advisors, and accountability partners can also be a valuable way to discern God's will for our careers. These individuals can offer godly perspectives, prayer support, and practical advice based on their own experiences and insights.

However, it's important to remember that while the counsel of others can be helpful, it is ultimately our responsibility to seek God's guidance and make decisions that align with His purposes for our lives. We should not simply rely on the opinions or expectations of others but rather use their input as one of many factors in our discernment process.

Discerning God's will for our careers is not always easy or straightforward, but it is a crucial part of our journey of faith and obedience. By consistently seeking His guidance through prayer, Scripture, and wise counsel, we can cultivate a deeper sense of purpose, direction, and alignment with His plans for our lives.

❖ Trusting in God's direction for our careers means letting go of our own need for control and certainty and recognizing that His ways are often beyond our understanding or expectations.

❖ We can seek and follow God's guidance in our career decisions through consistent prayer, studying and meditating on Scripture, seeking wise counsel from trusted mentors and advisors, paying attention to our passions and gifts, and being open to God's surprising and unconventional plans.

❖ Discerning God's will for our careers requires a posture of humility, receptivity, and willingness to follow where He leads, even when the path is unclear or uncomfortable.

❖ Prayer, Scripture, and wise counsel are powerful tools for discerning God's will. Still, ultimately, it is our responsibility to seek His guidance and make decisions that align with His purposes for our lives.

❖ Trusting in God's direction for our careers is an ongoing journey of faith and obedience, but it can lead to greater fulfillment, impact, and alignment with His purposes for our lives.

As I reflect on my journey of seeking and following God's direction in my career, I am reminded of the many twists and turns, surprises and setbacks, joys and challenges that have marked my path thus far. There have been times when I felt confident and clear about God's plans for my life and other times when I felt lost, confused, or even discouraged.

Through it all, I have learned to lean into my faith and trust that God is always working behind the scenes, weaving together the threads of my story into a beautiful tapestry that reflects His purposes and glory. I have seen Him open doors that I never could have imagined and close others that I thought were perfect for me. I have felt His gentle nudges and whispers, guiding me towards opportunities and relationships that have stretched me, challenged me, and ultimately fulfilled me in ways I never could have planned on my own.

I have also learned the importance of surrendering my own plans and preferences and being willing to follow God's lead, even when it feels risky, uncomfortable, or counterintuitive. I have had to let go of my own definitions of success and significance and embrace a deeper understanding of what it means to live a life of purpose, service, and obedience to God.

As a minority woman in leadership, this journey has not always been easy. I have faced my share of doubts, fears, and obstacles, both external and internal. I have struggled with imposter syndrome, discrimination, and the pressure to prove myself in a world that often undervalues or overlooks the contributions of women of color.

Amidst through it all, I have also discovered the incredible power and potential that comes from aligning my career with God's purposes and plans. When I trust in His direction and guidance, I am able to tap into a source of strength, wisdom, and resilience that goes beyond my abilities or efforts. I am able to see challenges and setbacks as opportunities for growth and learning and to approach my work with a sense of joy, gratitude, and purpose that transcends the ups and downs of my circumstances.

Perhaps most importantly, I have discovered the deep sense of peace and fulfillment that comes from knowing that my career is not just about achieving my own goals or aspirations but about using my gifts and talents to serve God and others and to make a positive impact on the world.

So, my dear sisters, as you navigate your career journeys and seek to discern God's will and direction for your lives, I encourage you to lean into your faith and trust in His goodness and sovereignty. Embrace the adventure and uncertainty of following where He leads, even when the path is unclear or uncomfortable.

Cultivate a consistent practice of prayer, scripture study, and seeking wise counsel, and be open to the surprising and unconventional ways that God may guide and direct your steps. Pay attention to the passions, gifts, and opportunities that He has given you, and look for ways to use them to serve others and make a difference in the world.

Above all, remember that your career is not just about achieving external markers of success or significance but about aligning your life with God's purposes and plans and experiencing the joy, peace, and fulfillment that comes from living out your unique calling and contribution.

As minority women in leadership, we have a powerful opportunity and responsibility to be a light and a witness in our workplaces, communities, and the world. We can show others what it looks like to trust in God's direction and guidance, even in the face of challenges and obstacles. We can model a different kind of leadership, one that is grounded in faith, service, and a deep commitment to using our gifts and talents for the greater good.

So, let us step out in faith and obedience, trusting that God is directing our steps and guiding our paths. Let us seek His wisdom and guidance in every decision and opportunity and be willing to follow where He leads, even when it takes us beyond our comfort zones or expectations.

Let us support and encourage one another along the way, celebrating each woman's unique journeys and contributions and cheering each other on as we pursue God's purposes and plans for our lives.

Remember, you are not alone in this journey. You are part of a sisterhood of faith, a community of women who are seeking to live out their callings with courage, compassion, and conviction. You are loved and guided by a God who has created you for a purpose and who is working all things together for your good and His glory.

Take heart, my dear sisters. Trust in God's direction for your career path, and step out in faith to follow where He leads. The journey may not always be easy, but it will always be worth it as you discover the incredible plans and purposes that He has in store for you.

How to Seek and Follow God's guidance in Your Career Decisions

Seeking and adhering to divine guidance in professional decisions is a fundamental aspect of harmonizing one's career trajectory with their spiritual beliefs. This process necessitates proactively seeking God's wisdom and direction through various avenues, including prayer, scriptural study, soliciting sensible advice, and being attentive to one's God-given passions and talents.

Prayer serves as a crucial instrument in discerning God's will for one's professional life. By dedicating time to commune with the Almighty, individuals can express their aspirations, apprehensions, and desires while attentively listening to His voice and guidance. This practice involves not only petitioning for specific outcomes or opportunities but also imploring wisdom, discernment, and clarity in the decision-making process. Maintaining unwavering faith that God hears these prayers and is working behind the scenes to guide and direct one's path is paramount, even when the way forward may not be immediately apparent.

Engaging in scriptural study and meditation is another essential means of seeking divine guidance. The Bible serves as an abundant reservoir of wisdom, guidance, and inspiration for every facet of life, including career choices. By regularly immersing oneself in the study and contemplation of scripture, individuals can cultivate a more profound understanding of God's character, purposes, and plans for their lives. Biblical narratives of individuals who demonstrated faith and obedience in the face of adversity can provide encouragement and direction. At the same time, scriptural principles and promises can be applied to specific career decisions and challenges.

Soliciting wise counsel from trusted mentors and advisors is another invaluable approach to gaining insight and direction in professional decisions. God often communicates through the wisdom and guidance of others, particularly those who are further along in their faith and career journeys. Cultivating a diverse network of mentors and advisors, both within and outside of one's industry or organization, can provide a wide range of perspectives and experiences to draw from. When seeking counsel, it is crucial to be transparent and forthright about one's goals, concerns, and decision-making process while carefully weighing feedback and advice in light of God's Word and one's discernment.

Being attentive to one's passions, gifts, and opportunities can also serve as indicators of God's purposes and plans for one's career. By recognizing the pursuits that elicit joy, energy, and a sense of meaning and impact, individuals can begin to discern the areas where God may be calling them to invest their time and talents. Seeking out roles and projects that align with these passions and strengths can lead to a greater sense of fulfillment and impact in one's work. However, it is also essential to remain open to God's surprising and unconventional plans, which may involve stepping out in faith and obedience into areas outside of one's comfort zone or expertise.

Ultimately, seeking and adhering to divine guidance in career decisions is an ongoing journey of faith and obedience. It requires a posture of humility, receptivity, and willingness to follow where

He leads, even when the path ahead may be unclear or uncomfortable. By prioritizing prayer, scriptural study, wise counsel, and attunement to passions and gifts, individuals can discern and walk in God's perfect will for their lives and work. This approach to career decision-making brings a profound sense of peace and purpose, knowing that one's professional path is not merely about achieving personal goals or advancing self-interests but about aligning with God's greater plans and purposes. As individuals seek to honor God in every decision and opportunity, they can trust that He will guide and empower them to make a lasting impact and leave a legacy that brings Him glory.

CHAPTER EIGHT

Let Your Feet Do The Walking And Your Mind Do The Talking

As I've journeyed through my career and life as a minority woman in leadership, I've learned that success is not just about having a clear vision or a well-crafted plan. It's about taking consistent, intentional action toward that vision and cultivating a mindset of resilience, positivity, and perseverance along the way.

In the previous chapter, we explored the power of writing a self-contract—a personal document that outlines your goals, commitments, and action steps for your career and life. But a self-contract is only as valuable as the actions that flow from it. It's not enough to simply write down your dreams and aspirations; you must also be willing to put in the hard work, focus, and determination to bring them to life.

That's where the idea of "letting your feet do the walking and your mind do the talking" comes in. It's a reminder that success is a combination of both external action and internal dialogue, of taking tangible steps towards your goals while also cultivating a mental framework that supports and sustains you along the way.

In this chapter, we'll explore what it means to let your feet do the walking and your mind do the talking and how you can use this approach to overcome obstacles, maintain momentum, and ultimately achieve your vision for your career and life.

Taking Action Steps to Bring Your Vision to Life

The first part of letting your feet do the walking is taking concrete, measurable action steps toward your goals and vision. It's about moving beyond the planning and dreaming phase and actually putting in the work to make progress and create results.

One key challenge many of us face in taking action is the feeling of overwhelm or paralysis that can come with big, long-term goals. We may have a clear sense of where we want to go, but the path to getting there can feel daunting or even impossible.

That's why it's so important to break down your larger vision into smaller, more manageable action steps. By focusing on the next right step rather than the entire journey, you can build momentum and confidence and avoid getting stuck in the planning or perfectionist trap.

Here are some strategies for taking effective action steps towards your vision:

- ❖ **Prioritize and sequence your goals**: Review your self-contract and identify the goals and commitments that are most important or urgent for you right now. Consider the dependencies and relationships between different goals and create a timeline or roadmap for tackling them in a logical and realistic order.

- ❖ **Break down goals into specific, measurable actions**: For each goal or commitment, identify the specific, concrete actions that you need to take to make progress. These should be tasks that are within your control, and that have a clear output or deliverable. For example, instead of a vague goal like "improve my public speaking skills," you might break it down into actions like "research and select a public speaking course," "practice my elevator pitch for 10 minutes each day," or "volunteer to give a presentation at my next team meeting."

❖ **Schedule and protect your action time**: Once you have your list of specific actions, it's important to actually carve out the time and space to work on them. This means blocking off dedicated time in your calendar, setting boundaries around your availability, and communicating your priorities to others. It also means being proactive in anticipating and removing any barriers or distractions that might derail your progress.

❖ **Celebrate and build on small wins**: As you start taking action toward your goals, it's important to recognize and celebrate your progress along the way. This can help build momentum, motivation, and confidence and reinforce the connection between your actions and your desired outcomes. Look for opportunities to share your successes with others, reflect on what you've learned, and identify new opportunities or challenges to tackle next.

❖ **Adjust and adapt as needed**: Finally, remember that taking action is not a linear or predictable process. You may encounter unexpected obstacles, setbacks, or opportunities along the way, and it's important to stay flexible and adaptable in your approach. Be willing to revisit and revise your action plan as needed based on new information, insights, or feedback. And feel free to pivot or change course entirely if you realize that your original vision or goals are no longer aligned with your values or purpose.

By breaking down your vision into specific, measurable action steps and committing to consistent, intentional progress, you can start to bridge the gap between where you are and where you want to be. But taking action is only half of the equation. To truly sustain and amplify your progress, you also need to cultivate a positive, resilient mindset—which brings us to the second part of letting your feet do the walking and your mind do the talking.

The Power of Positive Self-Talk and Affirmations

The second part of letting your mind do the talking is cultivating a mental framework that supports, motivates, and inspires you as you take action toward your goals. It's about recognizing the power of your internal dialogue and beliefs and actively shaping them to work for you rather than against you.

One of the most common barriers to success that I've observed in myself and others is negative self-talk—the inner critic or saboteur that tells us we're not good enough, smart enough, or capable enough to achieve our dreams. This negativity bias can be especially pronounced for minority women in leadership, who may face additional layers of discrimination, stereotyping, and self-doubt in their careers.

That's why it's so important to cultivate a practice of positive self-talk and affirmations—to intentionally counteract the negative messages and beliefs that hold us back and reinforce a sense of confidence, worthiness, and resilience in their place.

Here are some strategies for using positive self-talk and affirmations to support your action-taking:

❖ **Notice and name your negative self-talk**: The first step in shifting your internal dialogue is to become aware of it. Start paying attention to the thoughts and beliefs that arise as you take action toward your goals, especially those that are critical, doubtful, or limiting. Name them for what they are—just thoughts, not facts—and practice observing them with curiosity and compassion rather than judgment or attachment.

❖ **Challenge and reframe negative beliefs**: Once you've identified a negative thought or belief, ask yourself whether it's actually true or helpful. Look for evidence that contradicts or balances out the negativity, and consider alternative perspectives or explanations. For example, if you catch yourself thinking, "I'm not qualified for this promotion," you might reframe it as, "I have a unique set of skills and experiences that could add value to this role, and I'm willing to learn and grow in the areas where I have room for improvement."

❖ **Create personalized affirmations**: Affirmations are short, positive statements that you repeat to yourself to reinforce a desired belief or outcome. They can be especially powerful when they are specific, present tense, and aligned with your values and goals. Some examples might be "I am a confident and capable leader," "I trust in my ability to overcome challenges and setbacks," or "I am worthy of success and abundance in my career and life." Consider writing your affirmations down, posting them somewhere visible, or reciting them out loud as part of your daily routine.

❖ **Practice gratitude and celebration**: In addition to challenging negative self-talk, it's important to actively cultivate positive emotions and experiences. One powerful way to do this is through gratitude practice—taking time each day to reflect on and appreciate the good things in your life, no matter how small. This can help to shift your focus from what's lacking to what's already present and abundant. Similarly, celebrating your wins and successes and savoring the positive feelings that come with them can help to reinforce a sense of progress and momentum.

❖ **Surround yourself with positive influences**: Finally, remember that your internal dialogue is not just a product of your thoughts and beliefs but also the messages and influences around you. Seek out people, environments, and resources that uplift, inspire, and support you, and limit your exposure to those that drain or discourage you. This might mean joining a supportive community or network, working with a coach or mentor, or curating your social media feeds to focus on positive, empowering content.

By consistently practicing positive self-talk and affirmations, you can start to rewire your internal dialogue and beliefs to work for you rather than against you. But cultivating a positive mindset is not just about feeling good—it's also about fueling and sustaining your action-taking and overcoming the inevitable obstacles and setbacks that come with pursuing your goals.

Overcoming Procrastination and Maintaining Momentum

One of the biggest barriers to consistently achieving our goals is procrastination—the tendency to put off or avoid tasks that we know are important but that feel difficult, uncomfortable, or unpleasant at the moment.

Procrastination can take many forms, from obvious time-wasting activities like social media scrolling or TV bingeing to more subtle forms of avoidance like over-planning, perfectionism, or busyness. But regardless of how it manifests, procrastination can be a major drain on our momentum, motivation, and progress toward our goals.

That's why it's so important to develop strategies for overcoming procrastination and maintaining momentum in our action-taking.

Here are some approaches that have worked for me and others:

❖ **Identify your procrastination triggers**: The first step in overcoming procrastination is to understand what drives it. What thoughts, feelings, or situations typically lead you to put off or avoid important tasks? Common triggers might include fear of failure, lack of clarity or direction, overwhelm or burnout, or a need for perfection or control. By naming and normalizing your triggers, you can start to develop more proactive and compassionate strategies for managing them.

❖ **Break tasks down into small, manageable steps**: One of the most effective ways to overcome procrastination is to make the task at hand feel more approachable and achievable. This means breaking it down into smaller, more specific sub-tasks or actions that you can tackle one at a time. For example, instead of trying to write an entire report in one sitting, you might break it down into outlining, researching, drafting, and editing phases and focus on just one phase at a time.

❖ **Use time-blocking and accountability structures**: Another way to combat procrastination is to create external structures and accountability for your action-taking. This might mean using time-blocking techniques to schedule dedicated focus time for important tasks, setting deadlines or milestones for yourself, or enlisting the support of an accountability partner or group to help you stay on track.

By creating a sense of urgency and commitment around your actions, you can help to override the temptation to put them off.

❖ **Practice self-compassion and self-care**: Procrastination is often driven by negative emotions like anxiety, shame, or self-doubt. That's why it's so important to practice self-compassion and self-care as you work towards your goals. This means being kind and understanding with yourself when you struggle or fall short and prioritizing activities that help you recharge and manage stress. It also means celebrating your progress and efforts, no matter how small, and focusing on the journey as much as the destination.

❖ **Reframe challenges as opportunities for growth**: Finally, one of the most powerful ways to maintain momentum in the face of procrastination is to reframe challenges and setbacks as opportunities for learning and growth. Instead of seeing a difficult task as a threat or a burden, try to approach it with curiosity and openness. What new skills or insights might you gain from tackling it? How might overcoming this challenge help you build resilience and confidence for future ones? By shifting your mindset from avoidance to approach, you can start to build a more proactive and empowered relationship with your goals.

Overcoming procrastination and maintaining momentum is not a one-time event but an ongoing practice. It requires consistent effort, self-awareness, and self-compassion, as well as a willingness to experiment and adapt your strategies over time. But by committing to this practice and combining it with the power of positive self-talk and intentional action-taking, you can start to unlock your full potential and create the career and life you envision.

❖ Taking action toward your goals requires breaking them down into specific, measurable steps and committing to consistent, intentional progress.

❖ Cultivating a positive mindset through self-talk and affirmations can help counteract negative beliefs and fuel your action-taking.

❖ Overcoming procrastination involves identifying your triggers, breaking tasks down into manageable steps, using accountability structures, practicing self-compassion, and reframing challenges as opportunities for growth.

❖ Maintaining momentum requires a combination of external action and internal dialogue, and a willingness to adapt and adjust your strategies over time.

❖ By letting your feet do the walking and your mind do the talking, you can bridge the gap between where you are and where you want to be and create a career and life that aligns with your values and purpose.

As I reflect on my journey of letting my feet do the walking and my mind do the talking, I'm reminded of the incredible power and potential that lies within each of us. We all can dream big, take bold action, and cultivate a mindset of resilience and positivity in the face of challenges and setbacks.

However, we also all face our unique obstacles and barriers, whether they be external or internal. As minority women in leadership, we may face additional layers of discrimination, stereotyping, and self-doubt that can make it harder to trust in our abilities and worth.

That's why I believe it's so important to approach our goals and vision with intentionality, compassion, and community. We need to be proactive and strategic in our action-taking but also patient and understanding with ourselves when we struggle or fall short. We need to seek out supportive networks and resources but also learn to trust in our own inner wisdom and strength.

Most importantly, we need to remember that success and fulfillment are not just about achieving external milestones or accolades but about aligning our actions and mindset with our deepest values and purpose. When we let our feet do the walking, and our minds do the talking in service of something greater than ourselves, we tap into a source of meaning and motivation that can sustain us through even the toughest challenges.

So, my invitation to you is to take a step back and reconnect with your vision and purpose. What impact do you want to make in your career and life? What unique gifts and experiences do you bring to the table? And what actions and beliefs will help you bring that vision to life, one step at a time?

As you reflect on these questions, remember to be kind and compassionate with yourself. Celebrate your progress and efforts, no matter how small, and lean into the support and encouragement of those around you. Above all, trust in the power and potential that lies within you—the power to dream big, to take bold action, and to create a career and life that is truly authentic and fulfilling.

By letting your feet do the walking and your mind do the talking, you are not just working towards external goals but also claiming your agency and worth as a leader and a person. You are sending a message to yourself and the world that you are capable, deserving, and ready to create the change you wish to see.

So, let's take that first step together. Let's trust in the journey, even when the path is unclear. Let's lean into the power of positive self-talk and intentional action-taking. Let's support and inspire each other along the way as we work towards a world where every woman, regardless of her background or identity, has the opportunity to thrive and lead with purpose.

Remember, your vision and your voice matter. Your actions and your mindset matter. And most importantly, you matter. So, let's keep walking and talking, one step and one thought at a time, until we create the careers and lives we truly desire and deserve.

CHAPTER NINE

Becoming A Leader Of Influence

As I've progressed in my career and taken on various leadership roles, I've come to realize that true leadership is not just about having a title or position of authority. Rather, it's about the ability to influence and inspire others towards a common vision or goal, and to create positive change in the world around us.

For minority women in leadership, this journey of becoming a leader of influence can be particularly challenging and complex. We often face additional barriers and biases, both systemic and interpersonal, that can make it harder to gain credibility, respect, and access to opportunities. We may also struggle with imposter syndrome, self-doubt, and the pressure to prove ourselves in a world that often undervalues or overlooks our contributions.

Despite these challenges, minority women have a unique and powerful opportunity to become influential leaders in our workplaces, communities, and the world at large. By developing our leadership skills, using our influence to inspire and empower others, and embracing a servant leadership approach, we can create ripple effects of positive change that extend far beyond ourselves.

In this chapter, we'll explore what it means to become a leader of influence as a minority woman. We will discuss practical strategies and mindsets for developing your leadership capacity, using your influence for good, and leading with humility and grace.

Developing Your Leadership Skills as a Minority Woman

The first step in becoming an influential leader is developing your own leadership skills and capacity. This involves a combination of self-awareness, continuous learning, and intentional practice.

One of the most important aspects of leadership development for minority women is to cultivate a strong sense of self and identity. This means understanding your unique strengths, values, and experiences and how they shape your leadership style and approach. It also means learning to embrace and celebrate your diversity rather than trying to fit into a narrow mold of what a leader "should" look like.

Here are some practical strategies for developing your leadership skills as a minority woman:

- **Seek out diverse role models and mentors**. Look for leaders who share your identity and experiences and those who have different backgrounds and perspectives. Learn from their successes and challenges, and seek their guidance and support as you navigate your own leadership journey.

- **Invest in your learning and growth**: Commit to continuous learning and development, both in your technical skills and in your leadership and interpersonal abilities. Attend workshops, conferences, and training programs, read books and articles, and seek out new experiences and challenges that stretch you outside your comfort zone.

- **Build your emotional intelligence**: Effective leadership requires a high degree of emotional intelligence, or the ability to understand and manage your own emotions and those of others. Practice self-awareness, empathy, and active listening, and work on developing your communication and conflict-resolution skills.

- **Cultivate a growth mindset**: Embrace a mindset of continuous improvement and learning rather than a fixed mindset of innate ability. View challenges and setbacks as opportunities for growth and development, and be willing to take risks and learn from your mistakes.

- **Develop your strategic thinking and decision-making skills**: As a leader, you'll need to be able to think critically and strategically about complex issues and make sound decisions in the face of uncertainty and ambiguity. Practice analyzing data, considering multiple perspectives, and using a structured decision-making process.

- **Build your resilience and adaptability**: Leadership often involves navigating change, uncertainty, and setbacks. Develop your ability to bounce back from adversity, maintain a positive outlook, and adapt to new situations and challenges.

- **Practice self-care and boundary-setting**: Leadership can be demanding and stressful, particularly for minority women who may face additional pressures and expectations. Make self-care a priority, and learn to set healthy boundaries around your time, energy, and emotional well-being.

By investing in your leadership development, you'll enhance your effectiveness and impact and model a commitment to growth and learning for those around you.

Using Your Influence to Inspire and Empower Others

As you develop your leadership skills and capacity, you'll also have the opportunity to use your influence to inspire and empower others. This is where true leadership impact happens—when you're able to leverage your strengths and experiences to uplift and support those around you.

For minority women, in particular, this can be a powerful way to create positive change and challenge systemic barriers and biases. By using our influence to amplify the voices and experiences of other marginalized groups, we can help to create more diverse, inclusive, and equitable workplaces and communities.

Here are some ways to use your influence to inspire and empower others:

- Be a visible and vocal advocate for diversity, equity, and inclusion: Use your platform and influence to speak out about the importance of creating more diverse and inclusive organizations, and to challenge bias and discrimination when you see it. Be willing to have difficult conversations and take a stand for what you believe in.

- Mentor and sponsor other minority women and underrepresented groups: Share your own experiences, knowledge, and networks with those who may not have the same access or opportunities. Provide guidance, support, and advocacy to help others achieve their goals and reach their full potential.

- Amplify and celebrate the achievements and contributions of others: Use your influence to spotlight the successes and accomplishments of those around you, particularly those who may be overlooked or undervalued. Give credit where credit is due and help create a culture of recognition and appreciation.

- Foster a sense of belonging and inclusion: Create an environment where everyone feels valued, respected, and included, regardless of their background or identity. Model inclusive language and behavior, and actively seek out and listen to diverse perspectives and experiences.

- Empower others to lead and take ownership: Provide opportunities for others to take on leadership roles and responsibilities and support them in their growth and development. Encourage a culture of innovation, experimentation, and risk-taking, and celebrate both successes and failures as learning opportunities.

- Build bridges and create partnerships: Use your influence to bring people together across differences and build relationships and partnerships that can lead to positive change. Look for opportunities to collaborate with other leaders and organizations who share your values and vision.

- Lead by example: Perhaps the most powerful way to use your influence is to model the behaviors and values that you want to see in others. Be authentic, transparent, and accountable in your leadership and inspire others through your actions and choices.

By using your influence to inspire and empower others, you can create a ripple effect of positive change that extends far beyond your impact.

Servant Leadership: Leading with Humility and Grace

As I've grown in my leadership journey, I've come to embrace a servant leadership approach as the most effective and impactful way to lead. Servant leadership is a philosophy and set of practices that prioritize the growth, well-being, and success of others rather than the leader's self-interest or ego.

For minority women, in particular, servant leadership can be a powerful way to lead with authenticity, integrity, and purpose while also challenging traditional power structures and hierarchies. By focusing on empowering and uplifting others rather than seeking personal gain or recognition, we can create more collaborative, compassionate, and inclusive organizations and communities.

Here are some key principles and practices of servant leadership:

- **Put others first**: Servant leaders prioritize the needs and well-being of their team members, colleagues, and stakeholders above their own. They seek to understand and support others' goals, challenges, and aspirations and to create an environment where everyone can thrive and succeed.

- **Lead with empathy and compassion**: Servant leaders lead with a deep sense of empathy and compassion for others. They seek to understand and relate to others' experiences and perspectives and to create a culture of care, support, and understanding.

- **Empower and develop others**: Servant leaders focus on empowering and developing others to reach their full potential. They provide opportunities for growth, learning, and leadership and support others in their journey of development and success.

- **Foster collaboration and teamwork**: Servant leaders create a culture of collaboration, trust, and teamwork where everyone feels valued and included. They encourage open communication, diverse perspectives, and shared decision-making and build relationships based on mutual respect and understanding.

- **Lead with humility and grace**: Servant leaders lead with a sense of humility and grace, recognizing that they are not perfect and that they have much to learn from others. They are willing to admit their own mistakes and limitations and to seek feedback and input from others.

- **Focus on the greater good**: Servant leaders focus on creating value and impact for the greater good rather than just their own individual or organizational success. They seek to align their leadership with a higher purpose and mission and make a positive difference in the world around them.

- **Model integrity and authenticity**: Servant leaders model a high degree of integrity, authenticity, and ethical behavior in their leadership. They are transparent, accountable, and consistent in their actions and decisions and inspire trust and respect in those around them.

By embracing a servant leadership approach, minority women can lead with a sense of purpose, authenticity, and impact that goes beyond traditional leadership models. We can create more compassionate, inclusive, and effective organizations and communities and inspire others to do the same.

However, it's important to recognize that servant leadership is only sometimes easy or comfortable, particularly for those of us who have faced systemic barriers and biases in our leadership journeys. It can be challenging to prioritize others' needs and well-being above our own or to lead with humility and grace in the face of adversity or criticism.

Nevertheless, I believe that the rewards of servant leadership far outweigh the challenges. When we lead with a focus on empowering and uplifting others, we not only create more positive and impactful organizations and communities but also find a deeper sense of purpose and fulfillment in our leadership.

- Developing your leadership skills as a minority woman involves cultivating self-awareness, continuous learning, emotional intelligence, strategic thinking, resilience, and self-care.

- Using your influence to inspire and empower others involves being a visible advocate for diversity and inclusion, mentoring and sponsoring others, amplifying achievements, fostering belonging, empowering others to lead, building partnerships, and leading by example.

- Servant leadership is a philosophy and set of practices that prioritize the growth, well-being, and success of others over the leader's own self-interest or ego.

- Key principles and practices of servant leadership include putting others first, leading with empathy and compassion, empowering and developing others, fostering collaboration and teamwork, leading with humility and grace, focusing on the greater good, and modeling integrity and authenticity.

- While servant leadership can be challenging, particularly for minority women who have faced systemic barriers and biases, it can also lead to more positive and impactful organizations and communities, as well as a deeper sense of purpose and fulfillment in one's leadership.

As I reflect on my journey of becoming a leader of influence as a minority woman, I am reminded of the many challenges and opportunities that have shaped my path. I have faced my share of self-doubt, imposter syndrome, and systemic barriers and have had to work hard to develop my leadership skills and confidence.

However I have also had the incredible privilege of using my influence to inspire and empower others, particularly other minority women and underrepresented groups. I have seen firsthand the impact that mentorship, sponsorship, and advocacy can have on someone's career and life trajectory. I have been inspired by the resilience, creativity, and leadership of those I have had the honor to support and uplift.

I have come to deeply believe in the power and potential of servant leadership, particularly for minority women who are seeking to lead with authenticity, purpose, and impact. By focusing on empowering and uplifting others rather than seeking personal gain or recognition, we can create more collaborative, compassionate, and inclusive organizations and communities.

Becoming a leader of influence is not a one-time achievement or destination. It is an ongoing journey of growth, learning, and impact, one that requires a deep commitment to our own development and to the growth and success of those around us.

So, my dear sisters, I encourage you to embrace your journey of becoming a leader of influence, with all its challenges and opportunities. Invest in your own leadership development, and seek out diverse role models and mentors who can support and guide you along the way.

Use your influence to inspire and empower others, particularly those who may not have the same access or opportunities. Be a visible and vocal advocate for diversity, equity, and inclusion, and challenge bias and discrimination when you see it.

So, embrace a servant leadership approach, one that prioritizes the growth, well-being, and success of others above your self-interest or ego. Lead with empathy, compassion, humility, and grace, and focus on creating value and impact for the greater good.

As minority women in leadership, we have a unique and powerful opportunity to create positive change and transform the organizations and communities we serve. By developing our leadership skills, using our influence for good, and embracing a servant leadership approach, we can create ripple effects of impact that extend far beyond ourselves.

Remember… we cannot do this work alone! We need the support, guidance, and partnership of others who share our values and vision. We need to build networks and communities of support where we can learn from and uplift one another and challenge the systemic barriers and biases that hold us back.

So, let us come together as a sisterhood of leaders, a community of change-makers who are committed to using our influence for good. Let us support and inspire one another, celebrate our successes, learn from our failures, and challenge ourselves to continually grow and develop as leaders.

Let us never lose sight of the incredible power and potential we hold as minority women in leadership. We can shape the future of our organizations, communities, and the world at large and create a more just, equitable, and compassionate society for all.

Let us rise and embrace our calling as leaders of influence. Let us lead with courage, compassion, and conviction, using our voices and experiences to inspire and empower others. Let us be the change we wish to see in the world and leave a legacy of impact and transformation that will endure long after we are gone.

The journey ahead may not be easy, but it is one filled with purpose, possibility, and potential. With each step we take, each barrier we break, and each life we touch, we are creating a brighter, more inclusive, and more equitable future for ourselves and for generations to come.

CHAPTER TEN

Overcoming Obstacles With Faith And Resilience

As I've navigated my career journey as a minority woman in leadership, I've faced my fair share of obstacles, setbacks, and challenges. From systemic barriers and biases to personal struggles with self-doubt and imposter syndrome, there have been many moments when I've felt overwhelmed, discouraged, and even tempted to give up.

Through it all, I've learned that the key to overcoming these obstacles is not just having the right strategies or skills but also cultivating a deep sense of faith and resilience that can sustain us through even the toughest times.

Faith and resilience are not just abstract concepts or personality traits but powerful tools that we can actively develop and draw upon in our daily lives and work. They are the anchors that keep us grounded in our values, purpose, and identity, even when the storms of life threaten to push us off course.

Strategies for Dealing with Setbacks and Challenges in Your Career

No matter how skilled, experienced, or successful we may be, setbacks and challenges are an inevitable part of any career journey. Whether it's a missed promotion, a difficult boss, a failed project, or a personal struggle, we all face moments when things don't go according to plan.

The key to dealing with these setbacks and challenges is not to avoid or ignore them but to develop strategies and mindsets that can help us navigate them with grace, resilience, and a growth mindset.

Here are some practical strategies that have helped me to deal with setbacks and challenges in my career:

> ➢ **Acknowledge and process your emotions**: When faced with a setback or challenge, it's natural to feel a range of

emotions, from frustration and anger to sadness and self-doubt. Rather than trying to suppress or ignore these emotions, take time to acknowledge and process them healthily. This might mean journaling, talking to a trusted friend or mentor, or engaging in self-care activities that help you release stress and recharge your batteries.

➢ **Reframe the situation as an opportunity for growth**: While setbacks and challenges can be painful at the moment, they can also be powerful opportunities for learning, growth, and development. Try to reframe the situation as a chance to build new skills, gain new insights, or stretch yourself in new ways. Ask yourself, "What can I learn from this experience? How can I use this setback as a catalyst for positive change in my life and work?"

➢ **Seek out support and guidance**: When facing a difficult situation, it's important to remember that you don't have to go through it alone. Seek out the support and guidance of trusted friends, family members, mentors, or professional resources who can offer perspective, encouragement, and practical advice. Be willing to ask for help when you need it, and lean on your support network to help you navigate the challenges you face.

➤ **Take action and focus on what you can control**: While setbacks and challenges can often feel overwhelming and beyond our control, there are always things we can do to take proactive steps forward. Focus on identifying the actions and decisions that are within your control, and take small, consistent steps towards your goals and values. This might mean updating your resume, networking with new contacts, or pursuing additional training or education to build your skills and knowledge.

➤ **Practice self-compassion and self-care**: Dealing with setbacks and challenges can be emotionally and mentally draining, and it's important to prioritize your well-being and self-care during these times. Practice self-compassion by treating yourself with kindness, understanding, and forgiveness rather than beating yourself up or engaging in negative self-talk. Make time for activities that nurture your mind, body, and spirit, such as exercise, meditation, hobbies, or time in nature.

➤ **Celebrate your progress and successes**: When facing a setback or challenge, it's easy to focus on what's not working or what's gone wrong. But it's equally important to celebrate your progress and successes, no matter how small they may seem. Take time to acknowledge the steps you've taken, the lessons you've learned, and the growth you've experienced. Use these moments of celebration to fuel your motivation and resilience moving forward.

By developing a toolkit of strategies for dealing with setbacks and challenges, we can build our resilience and adaptability in the face of adversity. But true resilience is not just about bouncing back from setbacks, but about having the faith and inner strength to keep moving forward, even when the path ahead is uncertain or difficult.

How to Maintain Faith and Resilience in the Face of Adversity

Faith and resilience are not just about what we do in the face of adversity but about who we are and what we believe at our core. They are the foundations upon which we build our lives, our careers, and our sense of purpose and meaning.

For me, as a Christian woman, my faith is the bedrock of my resilience and the source of my strength in the face of adversity. It is the lens through which I view the world, the anchor that keeps me grounded in my values and purpose, and the compass that guides me through the storms of life.

Maintaining faith and resilience in the face of adversity is not always easy, especially when we are facing significant challenges or setbacks that shake our confidence and sense of identity.

Here are some ways that I have learned to maintain faith and resilience in the face of adversity:

- ➢ **Stay grounded in your values and purpose**: When facing adversity, it's easy to lose sight of what truly matters and to get caught up in the chaos and uncertainty of the moment. But by staying grounded in your core values and a sense of purpose, you can maintain a sense of clarity and direction, even when the path ahead is unclear. Take time to reflect on what matters most to you, what you stand for, and what you want to achieve in your life and work, and use these values as a compass to guide your decisions and actions.

- ➢ **Cultivate a practice of gratitude and perspective**: In the face of adversity, it's easy to focus on what's going wrong and to lose sight of the blessings and opportunities in our lives. But by cultivating a practice of gratitude and perspective, we can shift our focus from what we lack to what we have and find joy and meaning even in the midst of struggle. Take time each day to reflect on the things you are grateful for, the lessons you have learned, and the ways in which you have grown and developed through your challenges.

➢ **Lean into your faith and spiritual practices**: For those of us who are people of faith, our relationship with God can be a powerful source of strength, comfort, and resilience in the face of adversity. Take time to lean into your faith and spiritual practices, whether through prayer, meditation, worship, or service to others. Seek out the guidance and wisdom of your faith community, and allow yourself to be ministered to and supported by others who share your beliefs and values.

> **Surround yourself with positive influences and role models**: The people we surround ourselves with can have a significant impact on our mindset, resilience, and ability to overcome adversity. Seek out positive influences and role models who inspire you, challenge you, and support you in your growth and development. Build a network of mentors, peers, and friends who share your values and who can offer guidance, encouragement, and accountability as you navigate the challenges of your career and life.

> **Embrace a growth mindset and a willingness to learn**: Adversity can be a powerful teacher if we are willing to approach it with a growth mindset and a willingness to learn. Rather than seeing setbacks and challenges as failures or dead ends, try to view them as opportunities for growth, learning, and development. Be

open to feedback, be willing to try new things, and be willing to embrace the discomfort and uncertainty that comes with stepping outside your comfort zone.

> **Practice self-care and self-compassion**: Maintaining faith and resilience in the face of adversity requires a deep commitment to our well-being and self-care. Make time for activities that nourish your mind, body, and spirit, whether through exercise, creative pursuits, time in nature, or meaningful connections with others. Practice self-compassion by treating yourself with kindness, understanding, and forgiveness and by recognizing that setbacks and challenges are a natural part of the human experience.

By cultivating these practices and mindsets, we can build a deep reservoir of faith and resilience that can sustain us through even the toughest times. But ultimately, our resilience is not just about what we do or how we think but about who we are and where we find our identity and strength.

Finding Strength in Your Identity in Christ

As a Christian woman, I believe that my ultimate identity and strength come not from my abilities or achievements but from my relationship with Christ and my identity as a beloved child of God.

In a world that often seeks to define us by our titles, roles, or external markers of success, it can be easy to lose sight of our true identity and worth. We may find ourselves striving to prove our value through our accomplishments, seeking validation from others, or tying our sense of self-worth to our career successes or failures.

As followers of Christ, we are called to find our identity and strength in Him alone. We are reminded that we are fearfully and wonderfully made (Psalm 139:14), that we are chosen and beloved (Ephesians 1:4-5), and that nothing can separate us from the love of God (Romans 8:38-39).

When we root our identity in Christ, we are able to approach the challenges and setbacks of our careers with a different perspective. We can see them not as threats to our worth or value but as opportunities to grow in our faith, character, and dependence on God.

Here are some ways that finding strength in our identity in Christ can help us overcome obstacles and build resilience in our careers:

➤ **We can trust in God's sovereignty and goodness**: When we face setbacks or challenges that feel beyond our control, we can take comfort in knowing that God is sovereign over all things and that He is working all things together for our good and His glory (Romans 8:28). We can trust that He has a purpose and plan for our lives, even when we cannot see it, and that He will guide and sustain us through every trial and challenge.

➢ **We can find our worth and value in God's love**: When we face rejection, criticism, or failure in our careers, it can be easy to internalize these experiences as reflections of our worth or value. But when we find our identity in Christ, we can rest in the knowledge that our worth is not based on our performance or achievements but on God's unconditional love and grace. We can approach our work with a sense of freedom and joy, knowing that our value is secure in Him.

➢ **We can lean into God's strength and power**: When we face obstacles or challenges that feel beyond our abilities or resources, we can lean into the strength and power of God to sustain and empower us. We can pray for wisdom, guidance, and provision and trust that He will equip us with everything we need to fulfill His purposes for our lives (Philippians 4:13). We can approach our work with a sense of confidence and courage, knowing that we are not alone and that God is fighting for us.

➢ **We can find purpose and meaning in serving others**: When we find our identity in Christ, we are called to live not for ourselves but for the glory of God and the good of others. We can approach our work as an opportunity to serve and love others, to use our gifts and talents to make a positive impact in the world and to reflect the character and love of Christ in all that we do. We can find a sense of purpose and meaning that goes beyond our success or achievement, and that aligns with God's greater purposes for our lives and the world.

By finding strength in our identity in Christ, we can approach the challenges and setbacks of our careers with a sense of peace, purpose, and perspective. We can trust in God's goodness and sovereignty, find our worth and value in His love, lean into His strength and power, and find purpose and meaning in serving others.

> Setbacks and challenges are an inevitable part of any career journey, but we can develop strategies and mindsets to navigate them with grace, resilience, and a growth mindset.

> Practical strategies for dealing with setbacks and challenges include acknowledging and processing emotions, reframing the situation as an opportunity for growth, seeking out support and guidance, taking action and focusing on what you can control, practicing self-compassion and self-care, and celebrating progress and successes.

> Maintaining faith and resilience in the face of adversity requires staying grounded in your values and purpose, cultivating a practice of gratitude and perspective, leaning into your faith and spiritual

practices, surrounding yourself with positive influences and role models, embracing a growth mindset and willingness to learn, and practicing self-care and self-compassion.

➤ As Christian women, we can find strength in our identity in Christ, trusting in God's sovereignty and goodness, finding our worth and value in His love, leaning into His strength and power, and finding purpose and meaning in serving others.

➤ By cultivating faith and resilience, we can approach the challenges and setbacks of our careers with a sense of peace, purpose, and perspective and trust that God is working all things together for our good and His glory.

Reflecting on my journey of overcoming obstacles with faith and resilience, I am reminded of the many moments when I have had to lean into these practices and mindsets to navigate the challenges and setbacks of my career.

There have been times when I have faced discrimination, bias, and systemic barriers that have made me question my worth and value as a minority woman in leadership. There have been moments when I have felt overwhelmed by the demands and pressures of my role and have struggled to find a sense of balance and purpose in my work.

Through it all, I have learned to anchor myself in my faith and my identity in Christ. I have learned to trust in His sovereignty and goodness, even when I cannot see the way forward. I have learned to find my worth and value in His love rather than in my achievements or the opinions of others. I have learned to lean into His strength and power, knowing that He will equip and sustain me for every challenge and opportunity that lies ahead.

I have also learned the importance of cultivating a supportive community and network of mentors, peers, and friends who share my values and who can offer guidance, encouragement, and accountability along the way. I have learned to seek out positive influences and role models who inspire me to grow and develop and who challenge me to step outside my comfort zone and embrace new opportunities for learning and impact.

I have especially learned to prioritize my own well-being and self-care, knowing that I cannot pour from an empty cup and that I need to nurture my mind, body, and spirit in order to show up fully and authentically in my life and work.

Perhaps most importantly, I have learned that overcoming obstacles with faith and resilience is not a one-time event or achievement but an ongoing journey of growth, learning, and transformation. It is a daily practice of choosing to trust in God's goodness and sovereignty, finding strength and purpose in my identity in Christ, and leaning into the support and guidance of my faith community and network.

It is a journey that I believe we are all called to undertake as women of faith seeking to live out our purpose and calling in the world. Whether we are facing personal challenges, professional setbacks, or systemic barriers, we can trust that God is with us and that He is working all things together for our good and His glory.

So, my dear sisters, I want to encourage you to embrace this journey of faith and resilience with courage, conviction, and hope. I want to remind you that you are not alone and that you have a community of women who are cheering you on and standing with you in prayer and support.

I want to challenge you to root yourself deeply in your identity in Christ and find your worth, value, and purpose in His love and grace. I want to inspire you to cultivate a growth mindset and a willingness to learn and seek out opportunities for development and impact that align with your unique gifts and calling.

I want to encourage you to prioritize your well-being and self-care, knowing that you are a beloved child of God who deserves to be nurtured, supported, and celebrated in all that you do.

As we navigate the challenges and opportunities of our careers and lives, may we continue to lean into our faith and resilience, trusting in God's goodness and sovereignty and finding strength and purpose in our identity in Christ.

May we continue to support and encourage one another as a community of women who are committed to living out our calling with authenticity, courage, and grace.

May we continue to trust in the promise of Philippians 1:6, which says, "Being confident of this, that he who began a good work in you will carry it on to completion until the day of Christ Jesus."

For we know that our story is not over and that the best is yet to come. May we face each new challenge and opportunity with faith, resilience, and a deep sense of purpose, knowing that we are loved, chosen, and empowered by a God who is always faithful and always good.

CONCLUSION

Embracing Your God-Given Purpose

As I near the end of this book and reflect on our journey together, I am filled with a deep sense of gratitude and awe at the ways in which God has been at work in my life and career. From the early days of uncertainty and struggle to the moments of breakthrough and purpose, I can see the fingerprints of His grace and guidance at every turn.

Looking back on the lessons I have learned and the growth I have experienced, I am more convinced than ever of the importance of embracing our God-given purpose and living out the unique calling that He has placed on each of our lives.

Reflecting on Your Journey and Growth

When we take the time to reflect on our journey and the ways in which we have grown and evolved, we begin to see the bigger picture of how God has been shaping and molding us for His purposes.

I think back to the early days of my career when I was filled with ambition and drive but also with a sense of uncertainty and insecurity about my place in the world. I remember the struggles I faced as a minority woman in leadership, the systemic barriers and biases that often felt insurmountable, and the moments of self-doubt and fear that threatened to hold me back.

Nevertheless, I also remember the moments of grace and breakthrough, the people and experiences that God brought into my life to encourage, challenge, and inspire me to keep moving forward. I remember the mentors who saw potential in me that I didn't yet see in myself, the opportunities that opened up when I least expected them, and the sense of purpose and calling that began to take root in my heart.

Reflecting on these experiences, I am reminded of the ways in which God has been at work in my life all along, even in the moments when

I couldn't see it. I am reminded of His faithfulness and goodness and of the truth that He has a plan and purpose for each of us that is greater than we could ever imagine.

I am reminded of the importance of staying open and receptive to His leading, even when it takes us in unexpected or challenging directions. It is often in these moments of discomfort and uncertainty that we experience the greatest growth and transformation, and that we begin to discover the deeper purpose and calling that God has for us.

Encouragement to Continue Pursuing Your Career Purpose with Faith and Confidence

As I reflect on my journey of embracing my God-given purpose and aligning my career with His will, I am filled with a renewed sense of hope and determination. The path that lies ahead may be uncertain at times, filled with challenges and obstacles that threaten to derail my progress. However, I am learning to remain steadfast in my faith and confident in the plans God has for my life. I am coming to understand that my career is not just a means to an end, but an integral part of my spiritual journey and a powerful tool for fulfilling the unique calling He has placed on my life.

One of the most crucial lessons I have learned in pursuing my career purpose is the importance of maintaining a deep and unwavering faith in God's guidance and provision. In a world that often values self-reliance and individualism, it can be tempting to rely solely on my own strengths, skills, and knowledge to navigate the complexities of my professional life. However, I have come to realize that true success and fulfillment come not from my own efforts, but from aligning myself with God's will and trusting in His wisdom and timing.

This realization has led me to prioritize my relationship with God above all else, recognizing that my career is simply an extension of my faith journey. By continually seeking His presence and guidance through prayer and scripture study, I am able to gain a clearer perspective on the challenges and opportunities that come my way. When I am faced with difficult decisions or overwhelming circumstances, I turn to God's Word for strength, wisdom, and clarity. I have found that immersing myself in the timeless truths of scripture provides a solid foundation for my career, reminding me of my true identity and purpose in Christ.

Moreover, I have discovered that prayer is not just a religious ritual or a means of presenting my requests to God, but a powerful tool for discerning His will and aligning my heart with His. When I come before God with a humble and open heart, laying bare my fears, doubts, and aspirations, I experience a profound sense of peace and direction. I am learning to trust that God is not only interested in my ultimate destination but also in the daily steps I take along the way. By cultivating a habit of constant communication with my Heavenly Father, I am able to receive the guidance, encouragement, and correction I need to stay on track and pursue my career with passion and purpose.

Another essential aspect of pursuing my career purpose with faith and confidence is surrounding myself with a supportive community of like-minded believers. In the early stages of my professional journey, I often fell into the trap of trying to go it alone, believing that I had to prove myself and succeed on my own merits. However, I quickly realized that this approach was not only isolating but also limiting. I was missing out on the incredible power and potential of meaningful relationships and collaborations.

When I began to intentionally seek out mentors, accountability partners, and fellow professionals who shared my values and vision, I discovered a whole new dimension of growth and fulfillment. These individuals have become invaluable sources of wisdom, encouragement, and inspiration, helping me to navigate the challenges and celebrate the triumphs of my career journey. They have provided me with fresh perspectives, constructive feedback, and practical advice, pushing me to grow in my skills and character.

More than that, my community of faith has become a constant reminder that my work is part of a larger story, a grand narrative of God's redemptive purposes in the world. When I am tempted to become discouraged by setbacks or overwhelmed by the demands of my job, my brothers and sisters in Christ rally around me, lifting me up in prayer and reminding me of the eternal significance of my efforts. They help me to see my career not just as a means of personal fulfillment, but as an opportunity to serve others, advance God's kingdom, and bring glory to His name.

As I continue to pursue my career purpose with faith and confidence, I am also learning to embrace a posture of continuous learning, growth, and resilience. The world of work is constantly evolving, with new technologies, trends, and challenges emerging at a rapid pace. It can be easy to feel overwhelmed or inadequate in the face of such change, especially as a minority woman in leadership. However, I am coming to see these moments of uncertainty and discomfort as invitations to deeper faith and greater dependence on God.

Instead of shying away from new opportunities or difficult situations, I am learning to approach them with a growth mindset, viewing them as chances to develop new skills, expand my knowledge, and step outside of my comfort zone. I am discovering that the challenges I face in my career are not obstacles to be avoided, but opportunities to be embraced, knowing that God is using them to shape me into the leader He has called me to be.

This posture of learning and growth also requires a willingness to take risks, to step out in faith even when the path ahead is unclear or unconventional. It means being open to God's surprising and sometimes unexpected plans, trusting that His ways are higher than my own. It means being willing to let go of my own agenda and preferences, surrendering my career to His loving guidance and direction.

Of course, this kind of surrender is not always easy, especially when it involves facing fear, uncertainty, or disappointment. There have been times in my career journey when I have felt like giving up, when the challenges before me seemed too great or the setbacks too painful. However, it is in these moments of weakness and vulnerability that I have experienced the profound grace and strength of God most powerfully.

I am learning that true resilience in my career comes not from my own determination or willpower, but from a deep and abiding trust in God's faithfulness and provision. When I am tempted to doubt my abilities or question my calling, I cling to the promises of scripture, reminding myself that God has equipped me with every good thing to do His will (Hebrews 13:21). When I am faced with failure or rejection, I choose to view it not as a reflection of my worth, but as an opportunity for growth and refinement, knowing that God is working all things together for my good and His glory (Romans 8:28).

Ultimately, as I continue to pursue my career purpose with faith and confidence, I am discovering that my deepest fulfillment and joy come not from the accolades or achievements of my profession, but from a life fully surrendered to God and His purposes. I am learning to hold my plans and aspirations with open hands, recognizing that my ultimate goal is not to build my own empire or legacy, but to be a faithful steward of the gifts and opportunities God has entrusted to me.

This means continually seeking to align my career with His will, even when it requires sacrifice, humility, or obedience. It means using my platform and influence to serve others, to be a voice for the voiceless and a champion for justice and mercy. It means being willing to take the road less traveled, to pursue a path of integrity, excellence, and compassion, even when it goes against the grain of the world's values and priorities.

Reflecting on the journey ahead, I am filled with a sense of excitement and anticipation, knowing that God has great plans in store for me and my career. I may not know all the details or destinations of the path before me, but I am learning to trust in the One who does. I am discovering that when I choose to put my faith and confidence in Him, He is faithful to guide my steps, provide for my needs, and use me for His glorious purposes.

So I press on with renewed passion and purpose, knowing that my career is not just a job or a means to an end, but a sacred calling and a powerful tool for advancing God's kingdom on earth. I choose to embrace the challenges and opportunities that come my way, viewing them as chances to grow in my faith, develop my gifts, and make a lasting impact on the world around me.

As I continue to pursue my God-given purpose with unwavering faith and confidence, I cling to the words of the apostle Paul, who declared, "Being confident of this, that he who began a good work in you will carry it on to completion until the day of Christ Jesus" (Philippians 1:6). This promise fills me with hope and determination, reminding me that my story is not over yet, and that God is writing a beautiful narrative through my life and work that will echo into eternity.

So I choose to keep pressing on, to keep seeking His face and His will above all else. I choose to believe that the best is yet to come, and that He who called me is faithful and will see me through to the end. I choose to step forward with boldness and courage, knowing that I am not alone, and that my work matters deeply to God and to the world He loves.

May this journey of faith and purpose be a testament to His goodness and grace, a shining example of what is possible when we choose to trust in Him and follow where He leads. And may my career be a powerful instrument in His hands, a means of bringing hope, healing, and transformation to all those I serve.

Final thoughts and blessings for the road ahead

Coming to the end of this journey of reflection, growth, and discovery, I find myself filled with a profound sense of gratitude and awe. Looking back on the path I have traveled as a minority woman in leadership, I am struck by the incredible ways in which God has guided, sustained, and transformed me every step of the way. From the early days of uncertainty and struggle to the moments of breakthrough and purpose, I can see the fingerprints of His grace and wisdom woven throughout my story.

I am grateful for the challenges and obstacles that have stretched me, refined me, and driven me to a deeper dependence on God. Through the trials and setbacks, I have learned invaluable lessons about perseverance, resilience, and the power of surrender. I have discovered that my strength and confidence come not from my own abilities or accomplishments, but from the unshakable foundation of my identity in Christ.

I am thankful for the people God has brought into my life to support, encourage, and inspire me on this journey. The mentors, friends, and colleagues who have spoken truth, wisdom, and love into my life have been a true gift from above. They have reminded me that I am not alone in this struggle, and that there is power and beauty in the community of faith. Through their examples and their investments in my growth, I have caught glimpses of the leader God is shaping me to be.

Most of all, I am filled with a profound sense of awe and wonder at the faithfulness and goodness of God. Time and time again, He has proven Himself to be a God who keeps His promises, who is able to do immeasurably more than I could ask or imagine. He has taken my small acts of obedience and multiplied them into ripple effects of impact and transformation. He has used my unique gifts, experiences, and perspective to advance His kingdom and bring glory to His name.

As I reflect on all that God has done and all that He has yet to do, I am filled with a renewed sense of purpose and passion for the road ahead. I know that the journey of leadership and influence is far from over, and that there will be many more challenges, opportunities, and surprises along the way. But I also know that I serve a God who is sovereign, faithful, and good, and that He will continue to guide and empower me every step of the way.

So, as I look to the future with expectant faith and unwavering hope, I want to offer some final thoughts and blessings for the journey ahead. These are the truths, promises, and prayers that I cling to as I continue to navigate the ups and downs of leadership, and that I hope will encourage and inspire you as well.

First and foremost, remember that your identity and worth are found in Christ alone. In a world that often seeks to define us by our titles, accomplishments, or external markers of success, it can be easy to lose sight of our true value and significance. But as beloved children of God, we have an unshakable identity that is rooted in His love, grace, and acceptance. We are not defined by our mistakes, failures, or limitations, but by the finished work of Christ on the cross.

When you find yourself facing self-doubt, comparison, or the pressure to prove yourself, take a moment to pause and remember who you are in Him. Speak truth to your soul, declaring the promises of scripture over your life. Remind yourself that you are chosen, loved, and called by a God who knows you intimately and who has a purpose and plan for your life that is greater than anything you could imagine.

Secondly, cultivate a deep and abiding relationship with God through prayer, scripture, and worship. As leaders, it can be tempting to rely on our own strength, wisdom, and strategies to navigate the challenges and opportunities before us. But the truth is that we desperately need the guidance, empowerment, and perspective that can only come from a vibrant relationship with our Heavenly Father.

Make time each day to seek His face, to pour out your heart before Him, and to listen for His still, small voice. Immerse yourself in the living and active Word of God, allowing it to shape your mind, transform your heart, and guide your steps. Worship Him in spirit and in truth, declaring His goodness, faithfulness, and sovereignty over every aspect of your life and leadership.

As you prioritize your relationship with God above all else, you will find that He is faithful to provide everything you need for the journey ahead. He will give you wisdom and discernment for the decisions you face, strength and courage for the battles you fight, and peace and joy for the moments of uncertainty and struggle. He will open doors of opportunity that you never could have imagined and close doors that would have led you astray. He will surround you with the right people, resources, and experiences to help you grow and thrive in your calling.

Thirdly, embrace the power of your unique voice and perspective as a minority woman in leadership. In a world that has historically marginalized and undervalued the contributions of women of color, it can be tempting to shrink back, play small, or try to fit into the mold of what others expect of us. But the truth is that God has created you with a specific purpose and identity, and your voice and perspective matter deeply to Him and to the world He loves.

Your experiences, challenges, and triumphs as a minority woman have shaped you in profound ways, giving you a unique lens through which to see the world and a powerful story to share with others. Do not be afraid to bring your whole self to the table, to speak up for what you believe in, and to challenge the status quo when necessary. Trust that God has placed you in your sphere of influence for such a time as this, and that He will use your leadership to bring about His purposes and plans.

At the same time, remember that your voice and perspective are not just for your own benefit, but for the good of others as well. As a minority woman in leadership, you have the opportunity to be a role model, mentor, and advocate for those who may not have a seat at the table. You can use your platform and influence to amplify the voices of the marginalized, create opportunities for the overlooked, and to champion the cause of justice and equity in your industry and beyond.

Fourthly, cultivate a posture of humility, servanthood, and collaboration in your leadership. In a culture that often celebrates individualism, self-promotion, and cutthroat competition, it can be tempting to view leadership as a solo endeavor or a zero-sum game. But the truth is that the most effective and impactful leaders are those who recognize their own limitations, prioritize the needs and growth of others, and who build strong teams and partnerships to achieve their goals.

When navigating the challenges and opportunities of leadership, remember that your success is not just about your own achievements or recognition, but about the impact you have on those you serve. Look for ways to lift others up, to empower and equip them to reach their full potential, and to create a culture of collaboration, innovation, and mutual support.

At the same time, be willing to admit your own mistakes, weaknesses, and areas for growth. Seek out feedback and mentorship from those who can help you develop and refine your skills, and be open to learning from the diverse perspectives and experiences of those around you. Cultivate a spirit of humility and curiosity, recognizing that leadership is a lifelong journey of growth and transformation, and that there is always more to learn and discover.

Fifthly, remain anchored in your core values, purpose, and calling, even in the face of challenges and opposition. As a leader, you will inevitably face difficult decisions, competing priorities, and external pressures that can tempt you to compromise or stray from your convictions. In these moments, it is essential to have a clear sense of who you are, what you stand for, and why you do what you do.

Take time to reflect on the values, beliefs, and experiences that have shaped you as a leader, and to articulate the unique purpose and calling that God has placed on your life. Use these as a compass to guide your decisions and actions, and to help you stay true to yourself and your mission, even when the path ahead is uncertain or unpopular.

When you face opposition, criticism, or setbacks, remember that your ultimate accountability is to God, not to the opinions or expectations of others. Trust that He is sovereign over every circumstance and that He is using even the difficult moments to refine your character, deepen your faith, and advance His purposes in and through you.

Finally, embrace the journey of leadership with joy, gratitude, and expectancy, knowing that the best is yet to come. The road ahead may be filled with twists and turns, mountains and valleys, but it is also filled with incredible opportunities for growth, impact, and transformation. Every challenge you face, every lesson you learn, every person you serve is a chance to experience more of God's goodness, faithfulness, and power in your life and leadership.

As you continue to step out in faith and obedience, trust that God is going before you, preparing the way, and equipping you with everything you need to fulfill your calling. Celebrate the victories and milestones along the way, no matter how small or insignificant they may seem. Give thanks for the people and experiences that have shaped you, and for the privilege of being a part of God's redemptive work in the world.

Above all, keep your eyes fixed on the ultimate goal and prize – not just the temporary successes or accolades of this world, but the eternal joy and glory of knowing and serving Christ. Remember that your leadership is not just about what you do, but about who you are becoming in Him. Every trial, every triumph, every step of the journey is an invitation to grow in your love for God, your dependence on His grace, and your capacity to reflect His character and mission to the world.

As I close this chapter and look ahead to the unfolding story of my own leadership journey, I am filled with a sense of peace, excitement, and anticipation. I do not know what the future holds, but I know Who holds the future, and I trust that He is able to do far more abundantly than all I could ask or think (Ephesians 3:20).

My prayer for you, dear reader, is that you too would embrace the incredible calling and adventure of leadership with faith, courage, and expectancy. May you be rooted and grounded in the love of Christ, empowered by the Holy Spirit, and guided by the wisdom and truth of God's Word. May you lead with integrity, humility, and conviction, using your unique gifts and experiences to make a lasting impact on the world around you.

May you find joy, purpose, and fulfillment in the journey, knowing that your labor is not in vain and that your life and leadership matter deeply to God and to the world He loves. May His blessings, favor, and peace be upon you, now and always.

"The Lord bless you and keep you; the Lord make his face to shine upon you and be gracious to you; the Lord lift up his countenance upon you and give you peace" (Numbers 6:24-26).

Acknowledgements

I want to first thank God for placing this book in my heart and guiding me through the process. I want to thank my parents for their continuous hard work and dedication to my education and career. My sister and best friends for thinking I am way cooler than I am lol... and last but not least my daughter for being my inner voice and greatest gift I never knew I needed.

About the Author

Tekeshia is a dedicated and compassionate leader who brings over 15 years of experience in the healthcare industry. Growing up in New York City as a first-generation American to immigrant parents prioritized the importance of having a sound education and knowing your worth. Her humble upbringing has taught her the importance of community and encouragement for individuals' development. Through leadership roles, she has worked with and mentored women from all walks of life. She is focused on motivating others to become their best selves through personal and faith-based development to profoundly leave an impact in the organizations and communities they serve. Tekeshia has a Bachelors degree in Psychology, a Masters degree in Community Health Education, and a Doctorate degree in Healthcare Administration.